TO GOD BE THE GLORY. IT'S NOT ABOUT ME, AND IT NEVER WILL BE.

THE LORD IS KIND

Becoming Her

TIERRA MOORE
A DAUGHTER OF THE MOST HIGH GOD

IMPACT KATAV PB

The Lord is Kind

Becoming Her

First edition

This book was professionally typeset on Reedsy.
Find out more at reedsy.com

Contents

Prologue

I want to know who covers you.

Covered and no monitoring, stealing, killing, destroying, identifying or retaliation in jesus name. People really be out here and doing way too much.

Also don't be out here still killin and destroying, devil- it's dusty.

Y'all we are back at it- because I still didn't do the exact thing that Abba wanted me to the first time. It turns out- we had a miscommunication. First, this needed to be done in order (my fault there!). Second- it turns out that we deem as a 'testimony' isn't what Abba wants to hear at all. When we accept Jesus Christ as our Lord and Savior- He covers all of our sins. So technically- there's no record of the things that you've done or the places you've been. You're brand new.

> There's no need to testify to the old nature. It seems like a paradigm shift to me- but the thing we should note is that the shift can be shorter or longer than you think.

Now, not everything is brand new at once. I'm talking bout ya wounds bb. In fact at times this is a process. For instance my mind, needed to develop and heal to get to a point where I could speak without all the trauma coming through. That, in itself is a miracle to say the least.

I serve a God who does big and small things- even back when I didn't know Him as well- or when I wasn't taking my walk as seriously. Now, things are different- because He said that they are. Simply put- that's that.

Now- it's time for me to share the more intimate parts of my walk with Abba, but from the perspective of-who covered me? Yes, by focusing on who covered me, how He covered me, why He covered me- you realize that this book isn't going to be about me at all. Which was quite a feat to try to do when speaking in first person. In fact, it took an amount of healing to get this one through- to be able to show the Lord in these pages is a complete honor indeed.

Instead, it's about the Lord's kindness- and the ways that He, in His kindness has allowed me to experience it. This is of no works of my own- being human means that the fallen state is default. But, I serve a God that loves me so much, He sent His only begotten son, so that those who believe in Him will not perish but will have eternal life. That's on John 3:16. Biblical Facts.

His motivation- to bring Lovie Bear back into that sacred space with Him. In the Holy of Holies, able to walk with Him the way He intended. Intimately. Before I was in my mother's womb, He knew me- but because of experiences on Earth and my fallen state- I had to get to know Him again. But, the goal for Him was clear all along- to get through everything that happened to me. So I can sit on a cafe chair, drinking tea and recollecting all the times that the Lord is Kind to me. In fact the beauty of it is that I'm learning more and more about Him every single day- and you know what? His personality is so rich it doesn't even matter, He's always doing something new.

He wants you to know how Kind He is to you as well. This book is about you and Him, I'm just the vessel to pass the message along. The honor is all mine- truly. In fact, if no when- you find yourself in these pages- there's some insight on how to heal too. A jump start to mind renewal if you will. You'll come to learn that you operate differently from your God given identity in Jesus Christ once you heal. You get back to the person, and original design that you were before you were in your mother's womb.

That's the goal and intention. Just something to think about. In fact, once you get back to square one, you'll find out how powerful the original you is. I don't think I'll ever get back to square one. I get closer every single day, and that's the beauty of it. We have eternity to go.

I

The Covering of Becoming

There was a pivotal moment where I received a hint about who I was. It was after this phrase- "Welcome to the Illuminati".
How did we get here? The process began when I took my first breath. And continued with the ones that followed. Each one meant I grew, I tried, succeeded and failed.
I accepted Jesus Christ as my Lord and Savior- only to come to the realization that my covering came long before that.
Here's how Abba God covered me when I was becoming. And how He covers my being- even now.

1

Repent.

I was in deep.

Abba God looked down at me, as calm as ever.

I glanced around the room at the other girls in the cafeteria chairs. I'd been getting closer in my walk with God and- boom! Here were are. This was part of an ask of the Lord, but the reality of the situation hit.

One, I was really sitting in the den of the Illuminati. Two- the objective was to have me convert. I wouldn't.

Three- that left only one other option, to try and kill me. Apparently, the enemy knew more about me than I understood about myself. It turns out, they had a whole rap sheet of sin that I had been in. Every single one of those- was a legal right to end my life and never have me to return home again.

Heavy on the- girl what are you doing? You said too much, spoke too soon, tripped over your own words and now you're in the Lion's Den, and the lions are right down the hall.

"Have you ever heard of repenting?" Laughed the witch in a mocking tone.

Actually-no. I repented right then and there.

"We can't kill her, she's got a clean rap sheet. She isn't scared either."

"We can't even use fear to kill her? Ugh."

Then there was the consequences about this one being 'hard'. Y'all know how much we don't talk about repentance! We really need to- because I high key had not heard of repenting regularly. My walk with Abba God at the time- was full of mixture. In fact I had already had some close calls. That cheap little cafeteria chair felt different when I came to the realization that- if I HAD died on those escapades- I would have died. To clarify, died died and have been separated from God forever. Turns out, accepting Christ was enough to get me into Heaven- but there was power in actually walking the Word of God out on a daily basis.

That, meant that the mixture was going to have to go. But this also meant-that is was out of the Lord's kindness that I was alive to even make it to this moment. And the same kindness, is exactly what was going to follow me when I made the decision to walk this thing out.

No one really sat me down and told me that. That wasn't the only thing that I found out during that encounter. In fact, once I repented- the rap sheet dissapeared. However, the reading off of the rap sheet really had me sitting down and thinking about things. My family had these things called generational curses. At that point in my life, I came from idolaters, fornicators, adulterers, those that struggled with addiction. There was freemasonry, eastern stars and even other members of the occult. I found myself engaging in the same behaviors thinking that it was normal. But- what the world deems acceptable and what the Lord calls out are two entirely different things. That was something that until this moment- I hadn't really thought about yet.

I came back, came home and entered into one of the most traumatizing and painful experiences of my life. But look- even the Lord has turned that into joy! So, this is a testimony not about what I've done or where I've been (turns out Abba God doesn't like that- or Abba Bear as I affectionately refer to Him as :)). In fact, He found it annoying- so here we are- having a re-do. And I'm thankful and so grateful to Him that I'm alive and able to type this. Giving God the Glory, I wouldn't have it any other way. Now, I invite you to experience Jesus Christ and Abba Bear as my covering. Without the sacrifice of Jesus Christ, I wouldn't have been able to enter in Abba Bear's prescence cleansed of sin. And, without the protecting hand and covering of Abba Bear- I wouldn't be alive right now. Just know, they both want to cover each reader in the same way. For those that have accepted Jesus Christ, here's tips on how to be covered in your walk with the Lord. Here's how He covered my becoming, and now- my being with Him.

We've overcome the enemy by the blood of the Lamb and by the Word of the testimony. Revelation 12:11

See! We've already overcome- now it's time to walk this thing out. I found that the process of getting this to even be written was a tale in itself. There were bumps, snares, setbacks, issues, problems- learning. Might have even gotten bullied there for a second. But, we needed to have that conversation.
The conversation was why the fla-doodle I went and took the all the way around route. It came to my attention that- all of those failures were necessary. In fact, they were going to be so necessary because people needed to hear and learn from them. But, I had to get myself strong enough to navigate the ridicule

and the pain. I had to teach people how to heal, by showing and speaking about how the Lord took the time to cover me.

When you think about it- He has time to run the whole universe and still found a way to take the time to make sure I didn't get into too much trouble. I guess that's what you do when it comes to taking care of your baby girl- huh?

Parenting hehe.

II

Hello, Babygirl.

When I was younger we didn't attend church regularly. I didn't pray, or read my bible.
I played with barbies, ate blackberries and raspberries in the woods. Climbed trees. Fell from them. Played in construction sites. Did girl scouts. Gymnastics- and made sure my mommy didn't miss the flips on the big bars.
Abba wasn't part of my daily conversation.
But, He made it so He didn't have to be. In fact, His commitment to letting me know He was there, began before we would speak.
How Kind of Him.

2

Hello Lovie Bear, it's me.

Church was rare. My dad took us to service one day, it was a weeknight. Now, little kid me thought the option to stay up late was always a good one.

There was no kids church.

"Do we act like we're in the store?"

"Yes." My father replied.

My sister and I sat on either side of my father. My mother was nearby.

The pastor instructed us to turn in our bibles to the focus scripture. My father had two bibles- he brought the big brown one. He told me the big word that I had asked Him about was 'Amplified'. Okay. Then he had a smaller, leather bible that he carried around. I knew that one. His handwriting that was on the pages. That one was a ' N- eye-V'. I didn't know what that stood for.

My father flipped the pages in His bible, and came to the focus scripture. I crinkled my eyebrows with the realization that I had another question.

But, when I was in the store- I didn't have to whisper when I asked him a question. But, the big people were talking.

I tapped him on his leg.

"No I don't have to go potty. How do you know where to go in the Bible?"

His face softened when he looked at me, it turns out- this was a really, really good question to ask in church and not in the store. That was the night I learned about bible chapters, and verses.

I learned the book of Job, wasn't pronounced as Job- but as 'Johb'. My dad tried not to laugh, as I furrowed my eyebrows trying to figure out how could it sound so different when it was spelled the same?

My dad let me have a couple of test runs to make sure I got it. My sister did too. The rest of the time, I put my feet on the back rack of the seat in front of me and did some singing in my head while I played with my fingers. I looked down at the green carpet to pass the time.

That was the day, Abba taught me how to read His Word. John 1:1 states; In the beginning was the Word, and the Word was with God, and the Word was God.

This was the beginning. The first time Abba introduced Himself to me. Technically, He introduced me to the volume of the book that was not only the history of the creation of the world, but what was and would become the cornerstone of my very existence once I was ready. But even before I knew you could accept Him- He was still fueling every breath.

It was another weeknight.

I would get awful stomachaches from time to time as a little kid. Oftentimes, my mother and father would take turns rubbing my tummy while we waited for the medicine to kick in. Tonight, my dad was holding me on his chest and walking in circles in the bathroom.

"It doesn't usually last this long." My mommy was in the hallway. You know that look mommy's give you when they're concerned, but don't want to scare you? She had that look right there.

"We should take her to the church. There's a healing ministry tonight. There's something there for her, I'm sure of it."

"What time does it start?" My mother leaned back to glance at the kitchen clock.

"Um, around 7 I think tonight."

"I'll grab the keys, we can make it in time." My mother at that moment didn't trust the medicine- she trusted God. That's not something she acted on much at this point in her life. My Daddy carried the bibles, mommy would look sometimes.

My father carried me in. I kept my eyes on the green carpet as we walked over to the pew. My father sat me down, and there were some people being prayed over.

I grabbed my tummy. The pain was a lot. My eyes began to water up, and my mommy looked over in alarm. "Should we just walk up or?"

"Daddy?" I looked up at my father and a tear went down my cheek. "Is God going to help me tonight?"

Just then the preacher paused, looking across the room like she was listening to someone speak to her. She had the same focus on her face like I would get when my mommy or daddy were giving me instructions.

"There's a little girl here. About 8 or 9. Your parent drove you. You have stomach pains...and you're in a pink shirt."

My mommy glanced quickly over at me and did a sharp inhale. We all looked ay my pink shirt. I tried to stand but I couldn't- so my dad picked me up and carried me. This was the first time that I saw the preacher up close- it's pretty different than when you're far away.

"She can't walk." My dad said, trying to keep his voice steady. I saw my mom's hand on his arm- she didn't know what to do right now but she was trying to keep her face steady too.

"Poor baby" said the preacher, and she placed her hand on my stomach. At this point, I knew that the medicine was taking far too long. I was upset, but one thing was for sure- Abba heard me. He wasn't Abba yet to me, He was just God. I felt my stomach begin too loosen.

"I can stand up now." I said. It was too quiet.

"Daddy, I want to stand up now- while she talks to God."

My father hesitantly set me down, and I stood up. The more the preacher prayed over me- the more my knots is my stomach loosened. I was warm in tummy. My mommy's eyes were full of tears, and my Daddy was trying to keep a straight face. He lifted his hands in praise, my mommy did too.

"How are you?" Asked the preacher into the microphone. She leaned it towards me.

I learned right towards it.

"My stomach was hurting so bad, but it got warm and the knots left. I asked if God could help me tonight and He did." I said with a smile on my face.

"Look at that gift of faith." Said the preacher with a smile.

I smiled from my throne room glancing down at my Lovie Bear. She was getting bigger everyday. It was time to start having personal experiences with me. Look at that gift of faith grow!

"God helped me tonight", I said to my parents as we continued back to the car.

I sure did.

You know, this was the first time I encountered Abba God. He wasn't Abba yet- just God. But in this moment I came into contact with one of His character traits. Jehovah Rapha. Also known as the God who heals.

Looking back, it wasn't by coincidence that He chose to reveal to me this part of Him first. In fact, He had an order to this. He made his first introduction, because it was this part of Him that I was going to be running into the most in life. Not that He isn't omniscient, omnipresent and omnipotent- because He's all of that and more. But- He had Babygirl meet the side that I was going to use later.

In fact, I encourage everyone to think back to the first time that you ran into Abba God. Who did He reveal Himself to you as? How did He reveal Himself to you? That's the hint. That's the clue. He's an eternal and supernatural being on mystery- but He's not complicated. He's straightforward. Sweet. Simple- in a good way. Simple in the best way. The way where all He wants to do is sit with you and say- "Come here."

3

Abba and Mommy

I clicked on the keyboard to the church's main site. Since my parents divorce- we lived with my father up north. My mother remained down south. However, the reasoning behind their divorce was the discovery of my mother's affair. Mommy and Dad tried to make it work- but it was rough.

Abba was with me during this time. It was in a different way. I recall when we had gotten the orders it was time to move. I had three days to pack up my middle school locker, say goodbye to my classmates- and transition into a new school and section of the United States. The Lord in His kindness, only had me recently go over the trauma that I had endured in this period. While I was going through it- Abba was kind.

I kept her mind. She didn't ask. I watched as many of the traumatic events went into her subconscious. I kept my hand on her- through the fights. When she was shaking from trauma in the emergency room section of the hospital. I watched my Lovie Bear be pulled farther and farther back down from the trauma that she endured. It broke my heart. But, I still sent sunshine. I sat with her when she would eat ice cream. When she walked the hallways of her new school. I still sent butterflies, and sent her friends to love on her.

She still sang in choir class when her spirits were low. I followed her when she would sneak off to the bathroom after class to cry. I spent all day telling Lovie Bear, that she was still my Lovie Bear.

But now, it was harder for her to hear me. To see me, to sense me. But- that didn't make it harder for me to love her.

In fact, now that I sit here and think about it- the kindness of Abba God- especially as Jehovah Rapha was the covering. In fact, Abba God covered me in many ways- with different methods but each one had the same motivation. And- that was love. That is love. And it'll continue to be love- isn't that what kindness is supposed to be revealing anyway?

Mommy didn't regularly visit us for awhile. It was hard when she did come to visit, it would only be for a small amount of time. We would cry a lot- really because it kind of felt like when we watched my mom screaming on the lawn when we drove away in the moving truck. I think that's also part of what made it hard. Another reason, my dad traveled for work my mother was the primary caregiver. So my mommy and Dad switched places in a way. This meant my father now had the primary care of four children. Thankfully, my grandparents were nearby to help him out.

My mother stayed with the man she had an affair with. Things, well- turned abusive. Mommy didn't know how to support herself- my dad paid the bills so she had a short time to develop her hobbies into a career. She mostly stayed at home with us. She was stuck for awhile.

When mommy wasn't visiting on the weekend- she would go

to the church with the green carpets. I didn't pray too much, but I'd talk with God about my mommy. I missed her, and things were hard sometimes.

I heard her. I heard her mothers prayers about her and her siblings too. Her mommy, my Robin, was realizing the extent of what she had done.

I knew what to do.

It was a Sunday at the church with the green carpets. A leader called out a specific situation that matched what my mother had been going through. "You've had an affair, been divorced, lost your children...and God still wants to turn it around."

Robin shrank in her chair, and felt so small, like everyone in the world was looking at her.

It wasn't the whole world. It was me, trying to come and get her. I couldn't force her to get up, but I can give her an option to come forward.

If there's one thing that love does- love and kindess give you the option to move in your freewill. And, if you're finding yourself in the pure love- you'll come to the realization that that the option will come with grace too.

She hesitated, feeling all the guilt and shame trying to pull her back into her seat. Getting up and walking forward meant, that everything the preacher just said was true. She didn't know the person on her left, or the person on her right. This was enough as is.

A lady looked her over and said, "I can walk with you if you're scared." And just like that, all of her fear was gone. That's what perfect love does. It casts out fear.

Robin left her seat, and started to walk forward. She didn't know what was going to be waiting for her at the altar. Was she going to feel even worse then she already felt? Was God going to meet her with open arms?

With every step, something became more apparent- it didn't really matter. At the end of the day, she was realizing a powerful thing. She wasn't a victim- and she had to take accountability for what happened if she wanted a different result. That was the scariest part.

With every step, she walked up the aisle to the pulpit and stood there. Her arms were raised in surrender, tears going down her face. She felt guilty.

The preacher calmly looked at her and said, "He wants to redeem you. He can restore your relationship with your children, with yourself."

That was the day my mother accepted Jesus Christ as her Lord and Saviour. That's the day that mommy got an Abba too, not just God. An Abba-God if you will.

This was the moment when God ensured that I would get my mother back- because she would be pursuing Him. In fact, Abba didn't care about her past- He didn't want that in the way. So much so- that He put the power of the blood of Jesus Christ on it. I will be forever grateful. That's when I started to get my mommy back. She started to regularly visit, became more independent, moved away from that abusive boyfriend- and found herself in Christ. I refer to this as the 'good space' because I had my mommy again. The mommy that Abba knew too.

The Lord is Kind indeed.

4

She's with Me

There were some concepts that I became familiar with at a young age. I found out where babies came from because of science documentaries I would watch on T.V.. How fast I needed to get out of the shower when camping, so the big spiders wouldn't have time to fall on you.

But, there was one concept that I became familiar with when I was sixteen. One that people would freeze up about when it came up in conversation. One that made people hesitate, pause. It made me come to the realization that despite how kind Abba God is- there were things in the world that weren't.

One of these things was death.

I know this is something that people don't like to speak on, or about. But it's something that at someone point- everyone has to go through. The day I was introduced to death- it was unexpected death. That's one of the hardest kinds. First, death is a standard event for humans. There are few guarantees in life, such as being born, the in-between stuff (that varies from person to person), and the end.

There is much speculation about the end, but for the record, the realm of the spirit and eternity are authentic.

How would I be here, and how would you be here if it wasn't?

See? the fairest of points has been made.

Often, humans try to state this as being absolutely real, and it exists whether you want it to or not. There are some things that we can't limit to human perception. There's even science out there that confirms that a transfer of consciousness occurs after death. You can look it up on a digital device. They'll even spell check it for you. We respect free will; I cannot force you to make choices of your own free will. But just so you know, eternity and the realm of the spirit is a forever thing, as the name implies. So, if you have yet to think about where your soul is going when you die, or if you've picked something that doesn't involve accepting Jesus as your Lord and Savior- I recommend out of love that you do.

As do I.

By this point, God went from the title of God to Abba. In all honesty, for a bit here I took Him from the position of Abba and put Him back as God. Worse so, His Word and instructions became suggestions, and not the law as it is. This is the point in my life where Abba and I went through it. Well, really I was going through it- and Abba was trying to figure out how to remind me that He was nearby.

We're not going to spend time focusing on the mechanics of how I went off course- we're going to look at who covered me through them. I'll throw in a hint hint with a dash of clue clue.

And in His kindness, it was Abba. It was Abba by the goodness of His character. It was Abba through the sacrifice of Jesus Christ, because if it were not for Jesus's sacrifice and the Blood of Jesus- I wouldn't be here. It was Abba's gift of grace. I didn't earn any of this, nor could any work I can imagine pay the price of what the Lord, in His kindness has done. And what, because of the simple reason of who He is- continues to do.

The throne room of God is a stunning and eventful place. God the Father sits on the throne, with Jesus situated at His right side. A multitude of cherubim sing praises while flying to and fro. A woman enters the throne room, shoulders back, hands placed politely in front of an extravagant purple gown that the Lord designed himself.

"Father?"

He turns His head and looks at her, full of love.

"Hello, Robin."

"Do my babies know that I am safe?" She furrowed her brows, "can you let them know?"

"Did I not grant your previous request? What makes you think that I wouldn't grant this one? You may boldly approach my throne. You're home now."

The altar of incense of the prayers of His people burned, leaving such a pure scent in the room. *"I will send them confirmation of where you are, and I will do something even more beautiful at an appointed time. For now, be content with your current requests and not be troubled by the well-being of your children. They are in my hands as well."*

Robin smiled and said, "Thank you, Father God." She waved over to Jesus, who waved back. The nail mark in his hand was visible to the eye. "Thank you, Jesus."

Jesus smiled because she picked him to be her Savior, and now, she has access to everything. Everything he though about her having access to as he died on the cross. he had to die for in order for her to have. See, without him, there was no way she'd be able to enter this close to the Father or even enter into heaven. No one would.

Robin went to exit the throne room, full of comfort, love, and peace, knowing that God is God. The grand door opened, revealing the stained-glass hallway, and Robin waved to the other angels as she slipped past to head back to the main doors. She then stepped back onto the streets of heaven.

That's right everyone. That's Mommy. I know you have many questions about this, so let's start with the basics. For the sake of this testimony, I'll tell you a couple of things. First, when it comes to my mommy, she's part of the story. She's not the focus of the whole story. Instead, this is one experience where I was first introduced to the covering of the Lord. This is the very reason why Abba and Jesus did what they did- so we all have a chance to reach this part. Being able to experience heaven first hand for all eternity.

And this, is just one way that He reveals Himself. But this is not the only place where the Lord revealed that He is kind; we'll be sure to get to those later. Truthfully, how can we not?

Precisely.

Whenever you see those italics, that's the Lord. Here, He'll be referred to as Abba Bear or Abba.

This is Lovie bear, Babygirl, or Lovie.

Das me!

He has some things He'd like to say. Sometimes He talks by talking, other times He talks by other information. Sometimes- it's thorough other people. He can use signs, confirmation- He's quite creative about this indeed.

So, really this book is about Him. The Lord deserves more praise, but He's never had the opportunity to speak this way. So, this book is so that He gets just that. I love you, Abba!

Now, the question everyone is thinking about- why was Mommy with Abba? She was just here a couple of pages ago- we can flip and it's right there.

Mommy had a baby with the abusive man. She got on her feet, got serious with God and moved out to be able to support herself- and Toot Toot. She was going to move up north- to be near us. She wasn't going to have to tell Toot Toot we were out on the school bus when he asked about what we were up to.

But- she didn't make it. The missing person's report went out 24 hours after she didn't pick up when I called the hair shop. Yet, even in this scenario, Abba was with all of us at the same time. Equally as concerned about how we were handling things, and comforting us individually in ways we didn't know we needed yet. In fact, it took a couple of years to come to the full realization of what He had done for us- even in times such as those.

At this point, Abba and I were not as close as we'd been. It didn't mean that He went anywhere, I was the one that moved. He went from being a place of comfort, to someone that I wasn't even sure wanted to comfort me. My defense mechanism was to build up a wall- because I was ashamed of myself. But He still wasn't.

The night we got the call- I'll never forget it. Abba was in the room- as He is in every room- watching over me to ensure that I was covered. We heard grandma on the other end of the phone wailing- and that's when we knew.

Mommy was gone.

My heart broke. I know people sometimes say this as a response to a thing- but in all honesty- my heart broke. I wasn't going to tickle my half brother's feet anymore and listen to him sing along to his favorite shows. My mommy wasn't going to be moving up here to live closer to us, but she was coming back in a casket. I ran into my room and wept.

Abba God sat at the end of my bedside- his prescence tangible and his look concerned. He knew that she was up there with Him. But I didn't. In fact- that night was a seed that I didn't even realize was there. My pride wasn't trying to let me address it- and that was the fact that part of me was mad with Abba God. In fact, at this point I didn't even refer to Him as such- it was just God. Thirty- nine years gone in a flash. Just like that. And honestly, some of my hope went too.

My sister and I sat looking at each other. Abba between us both as we spoke about who went where. Someone needed to stay here, someone needed to go help move mommy's things. I stayed put.

I woke up in the middle of the night entirely unsettled. Abba was there- that was the prompting that I needed to get up. So, I did and went down the hall to my father's room. I peeked through the door, and a younger brother of mine is sleeping near my father. My father is awake.

Wide awake.

"Can I sleep in here too?" I ask. He nodded, and I crawled into bed. I hadn't climbed in bed with my earth dad for years. We both sat in silence as one of my siblings wept in his room. Right now, Abba God was close to Him too.

"I'm so sorry you guys. I know things didn't work out with your mom, but I thought she was still going to..."

He can't finish the sentence. "I thought she was going to be an old lady."

I glanced over at my father, and scooted a little bit closer. "I forgave her for what happened such a long time ago, I'm glad that I did."

Something in me knew that my dad needed a bit of comfort.

"She got better. She started going to church again, like how she did back when we were little and accepted Christ".

My father did a sigh of relief, and I also did one as well. "We have hope; maybe she's run into Grandpa already." He smiled, and I did too. He then made a startled gasp and said, "I just saw your mom. It was a vision. She's beautiful, healthy, she's safe." That's how Abba sent comfort to my Dad that night. He was covering him too.

Now that I think about it- I wonder about what aspect of God my Father met that night. In all honesty- I think he met Jehovah Rapha too. I think in some way- we all did.

When I closed my eyes, Abba did the same for me. That's when I saw her. She was shining with a golden light behind her, smiling wide in a long gown. She had two babies on her hips. Now, there were a couple of things I understood at the time. I knew that when babies died on Earth, they went into heaven, including the aborted ones. I know back when my mommy was alive, she had asked me to look over my brothers while she went to the doctor for a procedure. That meant Abba was with the babies too.

My father went to drop me off at school a couple of days later. I thought that I was okay. My eyes went to the mini bible in the corner of the door, and darted back up to the window. Once my dad stopped the car, I felt my stomach flip.

I wasn't ready.

Is anyone able to articulate the emotional and physical way your body confirms you not being ready? Or when that things is so strong, that you're able to feel it in your spirit.

I didn't know when I was going to be ready- but at this point in my life I was not ready. I didn't know how to say it- I paused. The words wouldn't come out- they didn't want to come out.

My dad's eyes went back to me, my younger siblings were looking at me.

"You're going to school."

I paused, "But I'm not-"

"You need to be strong for your brothers."

She clenched up and grabbed her backpack straps. She walked into the building- her face taunt. In that moment, the covering that I gave her was different than the rest. In that moment- I covered her by not letting her feel the true emotional impact of the conversation. This was too much for her now, but we were going to get there later.

In fact, there were things that weren't for her to understand yet. So I covered her for her protection. I wasn't going anywhere, never wanted to.

My mother's funeral was a couple of days after Valentine's Day. It was raining, but the church was nice. We were all sitting in the pews, with my mother's casket on full display. Just then, a breeze came in the room. At first, I asked about the air conditioning because of how cool the room was.

Ah wait, the cool breeze like back in Genesis?

It was Abba God, letting us know that he was in the room. The funeral went by quickly, Abba sent the energy for me to get through this. He sat while I sang with my sister. Abba God gave me the gift of singing, and I used it in school. I didn't do much praise and worship as of late- but Abba still came. It was a tough thing to do- but we did it.

We went to the funeral site, and threw rose petals while they lowered the casket. The rain stopped.

The rain stopped, and sunshine came through.

The sunshine after the rain? That's a covering too. I felt Abba God sent rays of sun to kiss my skin.

That's comfort and covering too.

The rest of that semester was a blur. It went so fast- I wasn't too sure how or why. My bible sat in the car on the way to school. That was the time where, I didn't want to pick up my covering. The Word of God covers you too. I knew some Proverbs by heart- only a couple of them. But, they helped me a whole lot. Sometimes- I would recall them but that was about it.

And yet, this whole time Abba God and Jesus wanted to show the love that they have for me. Abba wanted to cover me, but He couldn't force Himself- He's a gentlemen. Jesus is too. So- Abba God does what He does- He gets creative.

Maybe, it's finding extra pocket money when the ice-cream truck goes by. Maybe it's that meeting that should have been an email, turns out to actually be an email. He's always looking for a way to speak with us if only they would be able to listen.

A big note in that point of my life- was the sheer fact that there were others going through some traumatic things as well. We were all learning about loss, the sudden and abrupt kind. It led to some healing conversations, and a competition trophy for placing as 4th runner up. We cheered even louder than the people who won first place. Abba God was cheering too.

He had us be each other's covering- it turns out we all needed something from each other. A hug, a pep talk- and sometimes a 'are you okay?' when you've been walking around pretending that you aren't. Those types of things.

That can be a good thing. However, I didn't notice my slip into idolatry because of this. I'll be honest- Abba God has strong opinions about idolatry that I hadn't learned about yet. That didn't excuse me from my transgressions, but at the same time I didn't take the time to alleviate me from my ignorance. It took years.

I'll be honest with you- He didn't have to cover me in this. Or in the relapses. The times where it snuck back up dressed in different fashion. It was hard. But His love for me covered it. I'm not saying that His covering was permission- but it for my mercy that He didn't take me out for that one.

But, Abba knew- and He still sat right in the same spot that He had been. He knew for the next phases in life- whether I asked or not- I wasn't going to be able to navigate this on my own. Plus, it's who He is! He's not into leaving or forsaking you, even when you can't stand sitting with yourself. Even when you just did something that went against HIs status. Again, it's not permission but it's for your mercy and your namesakes. He'll pull up a chair, He'd love to have the opportunity to talk about it you've just got to be vulnerable. Vulnerability after trauma can be a hard, hard thing indeed. Abba knows that too. But He'd rather you know that you have a safe space and place to run to.

See, there was more Abba knew that He wasn't telling me. One, for the reason mentioned above- I wasn't ready yet. The second was like the first- but it was because of my lack of spiritual maturity. That, meant that I wasn't ready yet to steward a thing. See, not picking up the Bible to read the Word of God was a snare. Not praying, another issue. But overall, withdrawing from God would have been detrimental had He not have decided to stay.

Abba knew my bloodline. He'd been thee since Adam and Eve and was taking a major track record. He knew what the enemy had planned for me. He knew the snares and setbacks- but even more so He gave me the power of the Blood of Jesus. The real question- was I going to learn how to use it? Was I going to know what's available to me as a daughter? The power and authority that I had? The pace to get there was set by Abba, but the steps were on me. And in that between time- the Lord covered me in His kindness. Because let's be honest, it took time for me to learn how to not wobble when I walked.

It's important to note, that doesn't mean that any activities I did in the middle were acceptable. It just means my mind was too small to be able to comprehend the when and the why of God. The Lord said what He said, and He said it with the same mouth that made creation. Yet, here I was under the assumption that my ignorance was safety. Which was wild to think about when I understood His role in the fabric of creation itself. That covering was paramount during this time- because He knew I wasn't well. And since He knows the beginning and the end- I was going to need all the help I could get to navigate this middle. And He did this willingly in grace. Because the day that you sober up, is the day you really understand the necessity of grace and not being guilty for needing it. When you heal, you see all the stuff you didn't even know you picked up on, on the way.

He covered me, even when He knew in my heart, I was mad with Him. Even when He knew I didn't know this myself. That's kind indeed.

Then, He sent us a love note. Abba gave us favor, so much we won an in studio performance with one of my mother's favorite artists.

Happy Mother's Day!

We both cried and told Him thank you. He was beaming. Then

came my older siblings graduation. It was an incredibly hard time for her. She was trying not to be sad when she went across the stage. Her classmates all stood up and cheered her on. She did a little jump and a wave. My dad exhaled in his chair.

Before we knew it senior year was here! It was time to be a dancing queen, in the words of that pop culture group. Y'all know how mentioning names in things is. Abba God sat by, watching me go through my senior year. At first- things were good. I walked up to school on the first day when it hit me.

This is my last time, I was going to be walking in a building by myself. Usually I was behind my older sibling since we were so close. But today, it was Abba God and I. I stood there, with a smile on my face- this was the first time I talked with Abba God. The first time that it wasn't just a thank you.

A big step.

A big step indeed to tell you the truth.

That moment, pretty sure a covering went over my senior year. Now, some may sit and say- how did you know?

I didn't.

At least until later, when you look around and you're like- that was nothing and no one but God. Turns out, senior year is a giant transition point. I needed Abba there, even when I didn't know how, or when to ask Him about that. But that's why it's so amazing, the fact that He never leaves. But, that always brings about the question on How to include Him in our life? Yes, it's important to have the covering, and we're grateful for it, but what about the one who covers?

Abba God needs some lovin' too.

With that- reality came in fast during homeroom. Prom

wasn't just going to be a word, and college applications were upcoming fast. Abba saw my face shift. That's what He was waiting on- I couldn't walk through this part by myself. I just didn't know that yet.

Folks parents were saving up for college back in Pre-K. It was crazy to say the least in all honesty. That was when Abba saw me come face to face with one of the most intense periods of my life. This was the first time I faced the strain of internal and external expectations. But, there was one factor that was thrown into the mix- and that was surrounding the impact my mother's passing was going to have on my senior year and college process.

Well, at first- it wasn't so bad.

Then one night I sat on my bed with my knees curled up to my chest. Abba God watched reality hit.

"Abba, what do I do?" I sat on my bed, bewildered. Abba sat with me, with a smile on His face. Jesus and Holy Spirit were hanging out with us too.

Ah yes, some quality time- and a genuine question.

Then it dawned on me- my dad had been saving social security- perhaps it was time to check to see how much was saved?

I knew what her and her father struggled with. They were more alike than they realized. The choices they made during the conversation, were going to be the deciding factor of how this went. Her heart already was going through so much, I didn't want her to think that she was alone. She wasn't.

I took a deep breath and went downstairs. No- it didn't go well.

I watched her trying to break the children's seal on the medicine bottle.

"Once a day..." I read the bottle, while trying to unscrew it again. I was failing English, which was the last course that I needed to graduate. Long story short, a teacher pulled the concern alarm- and here I was beginning antidepressents and anti anxiety meds.

I sighed. It popped open and I took one, then went to sit in my room again. Now, the teachers had me under a microscope at school.

She wasn't sure if she could trust me fully with this part.

You're right, I wasn't sure about this at all. And it was wild considering He was covering for literally all of the other parts. This was me getting in my own way to say the least.

The covering here- was a bit of a different seasoning blend to say the least. The blend here was favor. The favor for this section was different- it was my teachers caring so much that they said something. It was being able to get medicine quickly- and my dad having a fast response to the notification from the school. The other part of the covering was favor with my English teacher- who worked to make sure that I got my assignments situated on time.

Another part of the covering, which now that I think about it totally counts- was my father also being corrected about a choice that he made. It turns out, that making me head back to school so soon- was a seed for grief to take root. So, that was something else that needed to be taken into consideration.

In fact, when I turned 17- I did one of those long white collared shirt and high knee socks videos. I played the theme of the year, and then went into being reminded on the necessity of taking my old records off the shelf. That was a blessing, my 17th birthday because if depression had it's way- I wouldn't have made it. Abba God joined me in taking a record off of the shelf- between this and 60's music- we could jam for quite some time. Just a snapshot of what was going on in life, while true vulnerability with Him was a work in progress- we knew how to share a laugh. It was Kind of the Lord indeed to say the least.

I'd like to think that Abba God doesn't get a kick out of certain kinds of music. But, I know for sure that He does. While externally, I am young- internally the music of the 50's and 60's in on repeat. As long as it's pure- He's having a blast. Put on a boogie- some dance music. Grab yourself some disco praise (a personal favorite of mine). Keep it going- keep it moving. Keep Him in it- He invented dancing. I'm sure He would break dance in the throne room if He had the time.

Around this time came an uncomfortable topic of conversation. It had to do with the phrase that made heads turn- 'community college'.

Dun.

Dun.

DUN.

You may as well have yelled out some words from a coloring book if you said that phrase.

With the beginning waves of college acceptances, the comparison battle was on. One part of the comparison battle in high school, is that they don't have a formal sign up. Worse, the "You're better than community college argument." I thought that was the worst of it- and then boom it came. The one where folks assumed I was going to use my mother's life insurance money to pay for school.

I put in my headphones and closed my locker. It was a little aggressive. I turned up my emo indie rock and headed down the hallway to class. No one spoke to you when you had headphones in. Fun fact, later on I found out that there were spirits that can reach out to you in the music that you listen to. And in fact, worsen your mood. I was supercharging the spirits of anxiety and depression. They were doing the toxic tango- and I'm there just a bee-bopping along.

I covered her through that too.

Part of the reason why He covered me through that was because- you guessed it- I wasn't ready to process the totality of what happened yet. It turns out, Jehovah Rapha moves in appointed times too.

See, there's a difference between doing things out of ignorance, or subconsciously- and sitting there to actually plan something out. In a way, while my ignorance of that protected me from correction- it didn't alleviate or eliminate the effects from the music going through my ears. If anything- you'll see a recurring thing- that I genuinely did not know as much about Abba God as Abba God knew about me.

The thing is, because of Jesus Christ- I had the dominion and authority to overcome this. But, I didn't know the full detail in how to do that. We're going on a segway to have a conversation about Christianity- specifically American. We do the motions, but we really don't know how to use the tools and weaponry that are accessible to us in Jesus Christ. The full armor of God from the sixth chapter of Ephesians just getting dusty. And despite that, the Lord was still making the conscious choice in His kindness to cover me anyways.

But, my father was looking at me like- girl, that's your option. It turns out, there was no savings for college. My father was struggling with the reality of the situation that He was the sole parent of four kids. And, we weren't slowing down on growing up, and problems weren't dissapearing to say the least.

I have to be honest, you know how I mentioned that Jehovah Rapha-that character portion of Abba God- moves in appointed times too? Well I'm not saying my dad and I had the best relationship. I am saying that we both had out own appointed times to meet Jehovah Rapha. I'm not saying they were lined up, or linear, or they complemented each other all the time. In fact, I couldn't say that about my family- we all handled things differently. However, what was the most important was this. At the end of the day, Jehovah Rapha knew when we'd all need to meet.

It was more than just family. Friends. New ones, old ones. Old classmates. Old coworkers. People you meet in big and small conversation. People that you laugh with, people that you love, or people that cause you to rise in love. People who, at the end of the day may or may not actually like you. We all run into the character traits of Abba God at different times. Even- when He's just God to you. Or maybe- you don't believe that He exists- that doesn't mean He isn't sitting there and waiting for you to have a conversation.

Sometimes- I think it's not just time yet. It's not an excuse for abuse, or for mistreatment. But sometimes- people aren't ready. Just remember when you weren't ready too. And, give grace accordingly- but grace isn't an invitation to keep getting smacked in the face. You can take some scoots to the side on that one. But still- give them a wave.

My mother's funeral was near Valentine's day. There was a whole lot to get situated because of what happened.

III

The Ongoing Becoming.

Now- the process of Becoming. It began before my Mother passed. However, this part of Becoming- became after the shaking. The shaking, was when the trauma and pain felt closer than Abba was. When the enemy suppressed what made Lovie Bear- well, Lovie Bear. But- we're not focusing on the trauma. Instead- we're going to talk about the God that covers, and the God that heals me. The Abba God that came back for Lovie Bear- even when Lovie Bear didn't know who Lovie Bear was anymore.

It didn't stop

5

After the Call

It's Ringing

Abba God was with us when the phone rang. It felt like the phone was fast, and slow at the same time. We'd been waiting.

It was hours.

Hours.

Hours.

No one ate. No one moved. We didn't know how.

I didn't feel Him on the staircase. We didn't know the contents of the call- but He did. At this point in time- everyone's heart broke in a different way but we didn't find that out until later. Abba was here- and He didn't go anywhere. His word states the Psalm 147:3, that He heals the brokenhearted and binds up their wounds (ESV).

Wounds don't heal out the gate. Sometimes, this can go out in waves. It depends on how, when and in what capacity you allow Abba God to move. But, sometimes it's Him taking things in waves. He knows what you can handle, and when you're able to handle it. He knows about the subconscious things that can't come to the surface yet.

This was the night where the chain of traumas turned into a bomb. I ran up the staircase while Abba God reached out to all of us at the same time.

The biggest thing I didn't understand- was this a broken promise? Intentional? And the biggest question that I asked myself- where was Abba God when this happened? That was the day something went into my subconscious- it was that I was mad with God about what transpired. I didn't know it, but He did.

I called a friend. We wept on the phone.

I didn't call out to Abba God.

Not when my sister and I were discussing who went where.

Not when I thought about my half brother sitting at daycare.

I crawled into my dad's room, and scooted onto the bed. My other sibling was there. My dad was awake with Abba God- quiet and in shock.

My dad already forgave mommy a long time ago- but part of him thought my mommy was going to get to be an old lady. Even when it wasn't with him. He was fine with that. I let him know that mommy got better. She went to church again, and accepted Christ as her Lord and savior. My dad exhaled.

"We have hope- maybe she's run into grandpa already." My father accepted Christ as well. We knew this meant that one day we'd see each other again.

Just then Abba sent my dad a picture. Abba God loves to talk, sometimes He has to get creative about it when you don't know how or when to listen- or if you're going through it. He prefers intimate conversation though!

In the picture- mommy was like how she was in the throne room. Beautiful, healthy, happy and safe. We stayed awake chatting.

Abba sent me a picture too. She had two babies on her hips, and she was smiling. I was a little confused. I hadn't gotten a brain picture in awhile. There was a period of time- my mom's 'bad period' I call it. Abba recently had me speak about it in therapy. Shoutout to Holy Ghost filled therapists, for real.

The first day back to school was hard. Dad pulled up to the school, and my stomach dropped. Abba was with us, and glanced over at me. I hesitated.

My dad didn't react well. His worst fear at the time, were his children getting messed up. Now, I didn't have babies, but I know that you want what's best for them. This was what my dad thought was the best for me at the moment.

I spoke up, that I wasn't ready.

He said I needed to be strong and be a good example to my brothers. Emotionally, I hit a brick wall. I didn't feel safe with him. I felt safe with mom, but now that sense of safe was gone too. He didn't budge. This was the first time that I felt rejected. Abba was there, because He knows the hearts of men- from the motivation behind their actions to the wounds that you can get on the receiving end of them. None of this was a mystery to him. I grabbed the straps of my backpack, and slipped out of the car making sure the tears didn't fall. That's what strength meant, right?

In this moment, the Lord covered me from processing the full emotional impact of the situation. The moment slipped into my subconscious, but that didn't mean that the impact was lessened in any capacity. Subconscious things influence actions too- but what's important is addressing them when they come up.

Right now, Abba God knew that it wasn't the proper time-but at the time appointed we were going to speak about it.

Just- not yet. Besides, we weren't speaking like how we were- but He chose to cover me anyway. The Lord is Kind.

A Breeze

Funerals.

It's one of those things where you anticipate what's happening- but you're not sure as to what will transpire. You really just pray that nothing goes wrong, and it's a good day at the end of the day.

Abba God sat with us in the chapel. The lighting was peaceful and calm. They were speaking when I felt a brush of air over my skin. I asked my father if they turned on the air conditioner. They hadn't.

Abba God sent some kisses across my skin, that brush was a "I'm here and I love you." The air that I felt was a covering- of strength to get through the day. To be able to sing a farewell song. He clapped when we finished singing.

The car ride to the cemetery was quiet. The driver only asked some light questions. Mommy had thirty-nine years on earth. I was sixteen when she went to be with the Lord. But Abba is still with me- from the moment He created me in heaven until now. The best thing is, He's going to be with me forever. I just want Him to have a great time.

The rest of junior year was a combination of avoiding stares in the hallway, while navigating a new normal. The Lord in His kindness told me of the upcoming events-and emotionally I still shut down. He wasn't upset with me- part of Him was just disappointing- in love of course. This was a bigger shock to my system, and that's because I wasn't going to Him like He thought I would.

Remember how I mentioned idolatry earlier? That was the surface level of it.

See- if there was one thing that the trauma did was carve out these spots called voids. The voids ached. So- I would fill them with anything that I could get my hands on. Music. reaching out for people before I went to Abba God. There were other things that I fell into- some things were physical. Others emotional- to fill a spot that was Abba God sized. It was why I went through so many things- people. Places. Spaces. In ways that you think that you would- and in other ways that you wouldn't.

There are two things that we need to chit chat about. The first- how death works. Now, this is uncomfortable but it's important to note that in this case my mother's passing was an appointed time. Not all appointed times were positive- this one was part of being a human though. This meant, that she had thirty nine years on earth. This meant at this point, regardless of the method it was time for her to go.

The second- how you can fall into survival mode. Coming out of that thing is tough- but we need to have more conversations about the effects of trauma and your walk with Abba God. Part of the reason why He covered me through this, is because He needed me to know about this for later. I didn't know that at the time- but it was necessary for me to keep going. Survival mode was the place I learned about anxiety. It was the first place that I ran into depression.

Later on, I found out that survival mode was the place where creativity lapeed too. It wasn't that I wasn't creative- I just wasn't in the proper space to navigate it.

Instead- part of me was convinced that I must have done something to upset Him. Or somewhere deep down, He didn't want me anymore. That was the enemy using my mind against me. It took a long time to realize that, moving forward in life. Now when it comes to that conversation- we'll get there. Abba God looked into my heart, and while part of me was associating him with trauma that didn't remove us from the truth of the matter. The truth of the matter is this- that no lie from the enemy was going to keep Him from me.

If it meant, He had to send a breeze, or find another way to speak with me He would. His creativity was going to come through. Abba God doesn't know survial mode. It comes with being the Creator I suppose.

Absolutely.

I was, and am- still Abba's Babygirl. Even when I self-harmed- He would watch to make sure I was okay. In it all- He had the same response, "You can come sit with me." I knew my heart was broken, but I didn't understand how I was breaking His. Yet, He still sat.

The rest of junior year was a combination of avoiding stares in the hallway, and trying to navigate a new normal. I was wrapped in survival mode-little by little my personality began to shift into other places. While other portions began to retreat into my subconcious because to me the environment wasn't safe anymore. Even when Abba God was nearby.

A Quiet Mother's Day

Abba God- as busy as He is, was taking note about the things that were going on in life. Turns out, making time means that you still have a great bearing on eternity and time at the same time. I'm not equipped for that, that's for sure. Well, Mother's Day was a touchy subject. I didn't know what to do.

Abba God was doing His throne room thing when and mommy waltzed in. She was more than likely coming from the praise and worship room, wondering about what we were up to. It was almost Mother's Day- but she popped up in here from time simply because well, she had the time now.

"Can you do something to make it a little better for them? I know things are rough." See, mommy asked Abba God to let her know when we were upset. Part of her was concerned. Abba knew this; He knows everything, but confiding in Him is a form of intimacy.

I've got something planned. Fret not, Robin.

"Okay, Abba God."

Back on earth, I was sitting by the computer and looking out the window. The phone rang, and I picked it up. I heard my name on the end of the line.

I raised an eyebrow, "This is she." This snapped me out of trying to think about how to cope with Mother's Day.

"Congratulations!"

I thought I was getting pranked.

She wasn't.

I wasn't. My sister came into the room and looked at the shock on my face. "What's wrong!"

"We won an in-studio performance?" I said, as more of a question than a statement. She looked at me and raised an eyebrow. "We won an in-studio performance!"

"A WHAT."

That's when it hit both of us. We agreed at the same time that this was from the Abba God and mommy. It had to have been. I almost forgot that I had even applied. We had some time until May, but this was definitely a sister day. We needed some time, and with my sister's graduation coming up- I was relieved for her to have an event to look forward to. The Lord is indeed kind! :)

I thanked Abba God for the experience. I turned back and caught a camera at the perfect time. That means He heard me. This was a covering, a place of joy for me to meditate on. A life support for survival mode if you will. But, more importantly a reminder that He was, and is- still after His Lovie Bear.

We had kept everything quiet until later. When the news came out- things were different. People's face shifted, and some even admitted to being jealous. It perplexed me, that I had buried my mother and this comfort was a cause for jealousy? Turns out, this was a test run of the favor that God wanted to bestow upon me later. But, I needed to start thinking about what jealousy looked like. This was a covering too. I needed to understand to be able to build things upon later.

Before we knew it summer was here. This meant, one less of my dad's kids was in high school. This meant, it was my turn to be a senior. Now, I wasn't too sure about my expectations for senior year. In all honesty, watching my sister go through prom and graduation gave me a little bit of something to expect. However, part of me knew that it was going to hit different once we got into the ring.

Summer was strange, as I was accustomed to spending it with my mom down south. So, this summer I took it easy. We took it easy, because we weren't ready for family trips at the moment. Which, was fair. Abba and I became a little more acquainted, which we were both delighted about indeed.

6

The Dancing Queen

Senior Year. This meant, that I was set to be a dancing queen. Y'all know the music and the beats for that one.

Abba God and I were walking up the sidewalk to the main entrance. We had to pass the senior lot, and my classmates were pre-gaming senior years. The paint markers and car scribbles were in full effect. Usually, I would walk up to the main door by myself. See, the gap between my older sister and I meant two things. The first- my sister and I had always been a year apart. This meant, that for most of our lives- we'd share the first day of school in different locations. But, we'd also have them at the same school sometimes. We had a small gap, so we were right behind the other one.

On the first day of fifth grade, I walked into the elementary school building for the first time. In middle school, I walked into the first day of eighth grade by myself. Now, walking into my last year of high school- I knew that I wasn't alone. Now, I took the time to say, "Hi Abba."

Little did I know at the time, that while He was escorting me to the building- the Lord was preparing to cover me for one of the most challenging years of my life. But, He didn't tell me all that. Instead, He smiled and watched me walk a bit lighter. We weren't so far off now. I put my headphones in, and an indie band began to play. Sometimes, I wonder if there was anything else that He wanted to say back.

Homeroom

I'd been sitting with the same folks since I moved to the area in middle school. We sat down and looked at each other, and that's when things became real. The overview was what we'd seen everyone else experience these past four years. Powderpuff and homecoming were the main markers for the fall. The spring events meant prom. My table and I looked at each other with the realization that childhood was slipping away, and adulthood was coming.

I hadn't spoken to Abba God about adulthood. Or, the transition into adulthood. I may have thought that I had more time- but was this covered? How was this covered?

These questions went back into dormancy in homeroom. But oh goodness they weren't down for long at all. Now, college applications are a battlefield when you attend one of the top high schools in the country. Some classmates came from lawyers, bussiness, congresspeople- things are intense. So those kids, they were in the ring with the other kids trying to figure out who was going to come out on top. This was the first time I realized, my mother's death left me vulnerable. There are personal expectations and external expectations, and things begin to shift when you begin to compare your situation with others.

While some battles for Harvard, Princeton, and Columbia, the rest of us tried to figure out who was 'safe' and who was a 'reach'.

But, as I was walking from the bustop to my house- my stomach may as well of dropped into my feet.

Who's going to pay?

Oh.

See, the plan beforehand was using my mother's low income information to get the grant money and what not for schools. But, mom wasn't here anymore. The foolproof plan wasn't fullproof anymore.

This part, Abba God already knew that I was going to need a covering. But, the covering that I needed at this point in my life- I didn't even know what it was.

But, He knew.

"Abba, what do I do?" I sat on my bed, bewildered.

Abba sat with me, with a smile on His face. The whole squad was present as I laid on my back, looking up at the ceiling. My mind recalled my earth dad noting that He has gotten some social security from my mother on our behalf. Maybe some was tucked away?

That was the day Abba God covered my mind. See, I wasn't all the way back from the trauma of the previous year. This upcoming year wasn't going to help the situation. Abba saw the external pressure of comparison begin to impact my mind. It was quiet, but there was only so much I was going to be able to process right now. And in His kindness, He covered me so we could get through this next part.

The more I compared, the more that I slipped. I didn't see it, or notice it to tell the truth. That was the dangerous part. More so, I didn't take the time to really press in with Abba to see where the finances were going to come from. Instead, my mind shifted to what was physically available to me.

I still had aways to go in that area. Plus, I wasn't going to be able to escape these college conversations so was I just supposed to sit there and not socialize for senior year? That's one game of frogger that wasn't going to fly.

It was in this moment, I began to limit what God could do. He could cover my mind, yes- but now possible with Him things just seemed to be overall impossible. And, that wasn't because of Him- that was because of me.

This was part of the reason that I ended up being on pills. Anxiety and Depression were enveloping me, and part me didn't want to let them go. I didn't know how to grief, I knew I needed to be strong, but it all kept adding up. Abba God covered me, because I still needed a layer of protection from the trauma that was trying to mask the little girl that He knew in heaven. He made it so I didn't have to ask, how can you ask for Abba God to cover something or someone that you're not even sure still exists?

I was quiet on the first day back from therapy. My father was quiet in the front seat. All I could think about was that, I wasn't able to be strong like how he'd asked me to be. But then again, I'm not sure if either of us knew that strong meant.

This Isn't Your Place to Ask

We couldn't put off the college conversation anymore. I inhaled and went down the steps to meet with my father. The community college application was trying to have a staredown with me, and I was avoiding it's gaze. Whispering that phrase was the equivalent of dropping a bomb.

The conversation didn't go well.

The shoulder shrug of my father, along with the "you'll have to figure it out" was tough. But the fact his eyes were not moving from the TV screen was the final straw.

I'd like to say, that I kept my composure. I didn't. The bottom of the staircase, the anger came out. It didn't make him pay more attention to me.

The 'normal' I thought that I could have was not going to be there. The realization hit me in the chest on that one. But, Abba God put His hand out to take some of the blow. I couldn't handle all of it. And, that was incredible that Abba did that because I didn't feel the first step.

I did not know if I was angry or sad - or was feeling multiple things at once. My body hit the stop gap button; this was the 'too much' section of my mind. Abba looked down at me and the hard stop that He had set in place.

At this point, the goal was just to get upstairs to my room.

"Help."

The second step. I think, at this point, I was just focusing on breathing. Oh, I didn't take my pills today- and then my brain went back to the time that I didn't have to go on pills. So, was this from not having pills? Or was I getting this 'tolerance' that my doctors told me I might have? Pills weren't helping- in fact, the pain was still there. But guess what? Pills don't erase your humanity. This was my first run in with the spirit of past, comparison and pain. A trio that was took time to discover, articulate, and cast out.

Exactly. They also aren't made to fill voids. I am.

At this point, I could feel the handrail's cold metal- which was good. But the thoughts started to cycle- was this my fault? Did I mess up? Did I deserve this? I rehearsed my Father's mannerisms during the conversation. This was a simple choice for him, without any regard for me. No amount of understanding, no comfort- a critique and an 'it is what it is.' That was memory recall, working with the spirit of past and rejection to see if this was really, my fault.

The third step. Ah, here are the tears- they were starting to load. I didn't talk with Abba on the staircase- but He fastened his eyes on me. The heavy that I had wasn't just from the present situation- but all the quiet things that sank into my subconcious. The quiet things- the fact that part of me was convinced that I had a role in my mother's passing. And the quiet, but incredibly loud presence of survival mode and the role that it was taking on me. But, I didn't know that.

Abba God absolutely did.

In fact, as rough as this situaton was Abba God knew how this was going to turn in my favor. That's because I was going to get to know Him in a different way. This was the entry point for me to meet Jehovah Jireh- which addresses the part of His character that provides. I didn't have to really ask Him about provision- this was going to be new because He'd been providing for me all along. But now, it was time for a formal introduction to something that I had known my whole life- but hadn't known that I had known.

See Jehovah Jireh isn't just for finances. Jehovah Jireh is the same provider since I took my first breath. Everytime I sat down to eat, or to have breakfast- I was eating food. That was a part of His creation. When I walked down the street, and there was sunshine- that was from the sun He spoke into creation in Genesis. He had been providing the fundamentals of my existence since the day that I was born. It wasn't something I thought about, but that's the responsibility of being a Creator. That's designing things so well that they are able to run themselves. Isn't that what the human body does? We don't have to remember to keep our heart beating, or remind ourselves to breathe. Praise be to the most High for that one in all honesty. That's a covering too. So really, Abba God was sitting back and saying- if you let me expand my character of Jehovah Jireh into other areas of your life then I can cover all this too.

And that was the key, I had to let Him.

I had to let Him show how He loves me even more.

This is why Abba God is love. But, when you're not use to love this can look more scary than comforting. Love is a bright thing- love shows you the areas in your life that are covered with flaws and places that are in need of improvement. When you're used to those areas not being spoken about in love- it's scary. It took time for me to be able to admit that too. It was a pride thing.

A beautiful thing about the Lord, is the sheer fact that the sacrifice of Jesus Christ allows us to draw into further intimacy with the Lord. We get to know Him as love more. That's because, He knows who He made you to be. And He didn't put this universe into existence to think that you are unloved.

However, in this present moment I was beginning to struggle in love with loving myself. So- getting to know Abba God in this way was scary. We'll get more into that later.

Instead, I'd look back on the moments where I felt loved. Those were with Mommy and Toot Toot. I'd tickle his feet and then kiss his nose when he was finished giggling. It sounded so fat away. I can still see it. Mommy and I went on a late-night drive to get ice cream at the beach, the last summer when she was on Earth. Shug was sound asleep in the backseat.

Then the present situation became more apparent at the fifth step. I can see myself walking the hall. Zoinked me right out of the happy space. But the real question here was- why was I only able to associate my happy times with people and not Abba God? This was a question for later.

Abba God set another precaution on the fifth step- I couldn't feel all of this at once. My therapist called it dissociating— but it was my body going into self preservation mode. As I ascended my mind became quiet. In fact, so quiet I didn't reach out to Abba God. I sat there in that space and hit the next step.

Abba brought back the good memories on the next step. As I got to the next step, the memories of my mommy and Toot Toot came back in full force. My mom peeps her head in the bathroom while I fix my hair. She pops up next to me and smiles, "Hey, baby girl! Good Morning!" She waves her hand and smiles, so I see the gap in her teeth. I giggle. She puts her face beside mine and says, "Wow, your face is so much like mine now. You're growing up."

We both pause and smile as she gives me a peck on the cheek. Then, in the mirror, we both see a blur of my baby brother getting into something he has no business getting into. As fast as that baby moved, his curls stayed distinct. I laughed, and Abba giggled as my mommy dashed outside the room.

My hand touched the doorknob, and I had to focus to turn it. Once I entered my room, I shut the door and glanced up to the same letters over my mother's door back at her apartment. WORTHY, in those big white letters you find in the craft store. The tears came back quickly once we saw that one; my eyes welled up with tears, and I sobbed. I went to the corner of my room and stood weakly. I used to lie on the floor and talk with Abba years ago, but I hadn't done that in a while. As I fell, it was happening so slowly, but a whirl of the recollection of recent events, both positive and negative, began to fill my mind.

It was in this moment, I went back to the good period when Abba and I were close. When I was now old enough to get my eyebrows done, when we were at church down south. I saw us in the aisles when the Holy Spirit overran the service, and everyone danced and sang. The joy flowed through the aisles; you couldn't help but get up and dance. I grabbed the bottom of my dress to kick up my feet while the trumpets played. My mommy was smiling so wide she was beaming as she praised herself into a spin. The whole congregation was overrun. I remember my younger brother didn't want to attend the children's church that day. There he was, a complete ball of joy, praising the Lord. That period is the closest that I have ever been to God. To Yahweh. My Abba. Abba God. And you bet He was also probably busting a boogie with the angels.

And the thing was, He wanted these things not to be memories- but to be a present experience. It felt so far away, but He was not far away. In fact, He wanted us to get back to the space and He was already there. He hadn't left- I did. But here He was, sitting there. Patient. I began to weep when my body hit the ground.

"Abba..."

There was a whoosh.

The whoosh was a hello.

I managed to get out weakly between sobs: "I know that it's been a while, but I can't do this; it's impossible." The response was swift, almost like someone was watching me. "My mother and father may forsake me, but you said that you wouldn't." I cried even harder.

If you thought He was moving fast before, that quote from His word only increased the rate of His response. I stifled out a help before I felt myself crumple up to the floor. Then I sobbed. I broke. I was sobbing. Scared. I did the only thing I knew I could do. I knew He would hear me.

So, I called out for help.

"Help me please. I can't do this." I kept repeating, until I began to cry. That I was sorry. I was so, so sorry for everything. Even with that, I didn't know what to do about that either. I felt the last bit of strength leave my body.

That's an amazing thing about God, His strength is made perfect in your weakness. Right now, I was the weakest I'd ever been. Visually, nothing is there, but I felt a covering of comfort—of peace. That's Abba God telling me that He's here. It fell upon me like a blanket as I entered a deep sleep. It had been a long time, but having a touch from Abba is so distinct. You know that it's Him, and that's from the love that you experience. That comfort covering had pure love in it. And, I accepted it. Now, I entered into the rest that the Lord was trying to give me all along- to rest in His love and His strength in the spot He had reserved just for me.

Welcome Home

I woke up who knows how much later. The sun was at the point in the sky where you can't tell if things were going up or down. It was at this moment I came to the realization- He came for me despite me. The next feeling that I had was guilt concerning my distance from Him. It wasn't a justification for And it was at this moment I felt guilty about my distance from Him because of the events that happened to me. I was upset with myself; how could I go from such a space of intimacy to being so distant? The Lord had a right not to help me or want to convene with me. He chose to be understanding- especially with the content of my last outburst. He made my dad too. I didn't deserve it. But that doesn't justify the Lord's withholding- because of grace, He wants to love you more. See, one of the things Jesus did when He went to earth is that He had the human experience. God literally put part of Him in a person so He can have the full human experience and reconcile us back to Him. God is patient with us because He knows we're in a fallen state. But we can get back up again. Right now, I was down. And I knew it. And I said, and He heard me. But for now, we've got to work on getting back up again. Part of getting up is realizing the many things holding you down. Because them things that He tryna hold you down don't do a one time hit. I'm tellin' you.

Welcome home.

This new state of despondency was complex to walk out of. I won't say that the rest of senior year was easy- it wasn't. What did help to ease the situation was that I felt more comfortable talking with Abba about the things that were bothering me. It took me a minute, but Abba was a safe place for my fears. That didn't mean I was going to throw them all over to Him at once- but it was a first step. I could talk about my fears. At least, the ones that I knew about at the time. How I was really feeling, why I was really feeling it. But even the things I thought I 'knew' I was feeling were superficial or surface level. I was being intimate, but not intimate. He knew this, but that did not deter him from being there for me while I sorted things out.

Yet, here I was trying to find ways to disqualify myself from being worthy of His love. I turned my head and found the letters on the doorway, WORTHY.

Oh.

The Lord chose to be understanding- especially with the content of my last outburst. Abba God send a nudge- that He had made my dad too. Yeah, you're right- I didn't deserve for the Lord to meet me like He just did. It was because of His grace and mercy that He wanted to be able to love me more.

See, one of the things Jesus did when He went to earth is that He had the human experience. God literally put part of Him in Jesus Christ so He can have the full human experience and reconcile us back to Him. God is patient with us because He knows we're in a fallen state. But we can get back up again. Right now, I was down. And I knew it. In fact, I'm pretty sure I had carpet marks on the side of my face.

Yet, I spoke and He heard me. But for now, we needed to figure out how to get back up again. Part of getting back up again, was being honest about the many things that were holding me down- even the subconscious ones that I did not know about yet. Those things that were trying to hold you down don't do a one time hit. And in all this thinking as I laid upon the floor- I came to the realization that I had no idea how to get back up out of this one.

The situation, was still the situation and reality was the reality. But Abba God, was still Abba God. So, I exhaled and sat up and remembered I didn't put any water on my face. Which meant, that my eyes were puffed up. Gotta handle that first.

I won't say that the rest of senior year was easy. But, Abba was with me. I would talk with Him and He would listen to me. It took me a minute, but Abba was a safe place for my fears. Now, not all of them at once because there were some that I didn't know that I had yet. We took it (and honestly are still taking it) one step at a time. Even in that, He covered me from what I don't know and doesn't let me get hit with the totality of what I do.

I was being intimate, but not intimate. He knew this, but that did not deter him from being there for me while I sorted things out. The sorted out space, that's where the Lord wanted to go and where He wanted to get to. To Abba God, getting back to that space was the goal. Where He was home.

The process of getting Him to be home was going a process. But, that part was what mattered. See, the patience of Abba includes the process. If there is anything that you take from this book it's the importance of the process. Now we were going to address a smaller section of the process- a side quest if you will- about my coping skills.

For the record, the covering of Abba God here was so strong, because I didn't have great coping skills. Admittedly, as time progressed they would get better- but I'd pick up other ones that would be worse. It wasn't the best. In fact, some of my coping skills broke Abba God's heart. It's because many of them had me sinning and harming the very body He spent so much time creating for me in heaven. The one where He watched the system He designed grow my fingers and toes. The one where, the muscles formed so I knew how to kick and roll around. The system where, He created a container so my spirit being could walk the face of the earth- because the very system I would disrespect to comfort myself in my pain.

A disclaimer here- for self harm. That was my go-to for awhile. The worst part, was the thought that went into it. That was the hard part. Now, it was pills. Not too sure if pills were negative or positive- as things were intense for me and my brain chemistry needed help. But Abba wanted to provide a source of dopamine as well- in fact Abba has that supernatural joy- you can't find that in a bottle. That's the high quality stuff- this is the low quality stuff.

The thing was, part of the covering that Abba God also provided this year had to do with favor. I was failing the last course I needed to graduate- so that was part of the reason why I went on the pills. My guidance counselors and school were watching me like hawks. Which I needed. My dad gave them updates and they were sure to watch my tests and scores. They noted days when I would seem out of it- and they'd check in. I knew they cared, but sometimes it was hard to receive it.

In fact, it was tough in general with people and I didn't fully understand why. Abba God knew that rejection had taken a hold of me. I didn't fit in. In fact, this experience on earth was isolating. My college applications- I hadn't even started yet with everything else going on.

Part of me wanted to see that "I'm accepted", so that maybe I would feel accepted. This only revealed an identity issue, but my need for external validation was because of the presence of a void. The void that could only be filled by Abba God. I didn't want to talk to my dad about things, what if it didn't go as well as the car conversation? I didn't know how to be strong in the way he asked me too. The failure from that still stung.

But- Aren't You Good Enough?

Once we hit January, I couldn't hide at lunch anymore. People were asking about schools- I applied to a couple just to get it out of the way. One time, I got brave during lunch and ventured to mention community college.

The response, "But aren't you good enough for a four year?"

Ow.

The medication increased. As much as I didn't want to say this- the caption of this section became a meditation. Parents were excited, and kids were too. But, I wasn't sharing the same excitement. I wanted to though. I chatted with Abba God about it- and He knew how I felt. I was pretty transparent with Him about it- but part of me didn't want to feel how I felt. He covered me in that too. I wasn't ready to process all of this, but had to keep going.

And, this was the time period where I met my first actual boyfriend. If you look back at how broken I was, this was not a good idea at all. My grandma spoke to me about 'being in love' and all of that but I preferred books up until this point in my life. One thing that I should have one, which I recommend everyone do- is to speak with Abba God to see where people are supposed to go, and if they are ready to occupy that space. Part of the covering of Abba God, was the level that He protected me from Jezebel. Jezebel isn't a spirit that constrained to women, but you run into them in men too. It's who we refer to as a narcissist.

Narcissists, just like the other members of an enemies camp- love voids. If Abba God isn't there, then they've got space to try and to attach too. This was my first narcissist- and Abba God covered me in this as well. In fact, I was so ignorant of this- that I was sure I had found my husband.

I felt 'in love'- my grandmother said that this was good. The worst thing that could happen was a baby or an STD, in the eyes of my family. I didn't talk to Abba God about His opinion on the matter.

Abba's God's silence on a matter does not equate permission. In fact, I understood what He said in His word about these types of things- but it wasn't something I took as seriously at this point in my life. Later on, things changed.

Spring marked Senior week and the major milestones. College acceptance deadlines were coming up- everyone was full of chatter. I got an acceptance and a small scholarship. But, it turns out seeing that "You're accepted" at the top of the page didn't make me feel accepted. There was something else coming up to the conversation- and that was debt. There was so much buzz and conversation around college-no one was really talking about college debt and financial aid.

In fact, many people weren't going to realize the impact of debt until after we graduated. But it turns out, community college was going to be a covering from that too. There was a plan for poverty to take over- but Abba was guarding me from the enemy being able to gain access. See, I would have been borrowing from the cash flow of my future self- and that's something they don't tell folks about. This meant, that Abba God had bigger plans than what I had for myself at the moment. He needed me to break something in my lineage- that's for sure. But, another thing God does- is that He gives you what you can bear in that part of your revelation concerning you as well.

Options.

Well, the college stats were a series of rejections, on option to defer and an offer of admission that left a good 20k to come up with. As much as I didn't want to do it- community college was looking like the best option. There were a couple of other kids that realized that too.

On acceptance day, I wore a regular shirt. One kid got a t shirt from the community college and walked, shoulders back. One kid got into Yale, and refused to wear a t-shirt for his school. He didn't like the stigma attached to it, and was concerned about the other kids being bullied about it. The wildest part was a majority of us, never crossed pathways with this guy. He must have stayed in the advanced classes. But, graduation rehersal came and went. Prom came, I went with an old friend of mine- my dad wouldn't have a fuss over this friend as opposed to the guy I was seeing. But, this friend was at the time in the special friend category despite us being the same gender.

Nothing happened, but there was a thing. That was an entire conversation in itself- but I didn't inquire of the Lord to see how He felt about that one either.

My dad met my boyfriend, and his mother. It went well. Abba God was not proud of me after my first date- we'll just keep it at that. Yikes. He covered me here too. There were doors that were waiting to open while I began to explore certain things outside of wedlock. There was a reason why Abba God put certain boundaries in place- but I didn't inquire of Him as to why.

You bet He expressed Himself about this later on when I listened. Summer meant that there was a little bit of freedom before adulthood. I went on a senior trip, and rode bikes in Michigan with the girls I'd met in middle school. We didn't get closer until later- but we wanted to spend as much time with each other as we could before it was time to part ways. One was going to college near me, the others were going to other states. There was always the summer. And this was the one where we laid on reclined lawn chairs-waiting for the sun to set at 11pm, watching the cargo ships go by. With one of the clearest skies that I've ever gotten to see.

7

Community College Kid: First Semester.

The title of this section says it all. I submitted the application, and they got back to me fast. They don't tell you no. I signed up for one class- my grandparents let me know they were there for me to get my footing.

I thanked Abba God for the start, but I knew that I didn't want to stagnate. That was something that ran in the family, becoming comfortable. It was, go to work- come home and clock out kind of thing. That was the most common thing, paycheck to paycheck working for someone else. We didn't have many entrepreneurs. At least that I had heard of or saw. I recalled on earth, my mommy was resourceful but she never really moved into the realm of entrepreneurship. She had side hustles, Christmas wreathes, hair. But there was only so much that she got to.

I asked Abba God later on what the block was for her, and He told me it was because there were limitations on my lineage that no one had broken through yet. It's like the closer someone would get- the more that the enemy would try to knock them out of position.

There was something different about me. A tenacity, a stubborness (a good kind in this case) that didn't know how to quit. He built me like an ox. He made me stronger than what I could perceive or realize at the moment. This was a covering done in the kindness of the Lord, because I wasn't ready to know all about that yet.

Abba God and I learned how to ride the bus. The first day of school, Abba told me to let my grandma drop me off. I let her, and gave a slight wave as she yelled outside of the window for me to have a great first day.

The campus was more spread out, but it wasn't difficult to find the building. Something happened when I touched the door to enter into the building. It was Abba God planting a seed. I'd committed to a journey I knew little to nothing about, but I knew that Abba God was going to be with me. So- I was going to go.

"If this is where we start, then this is where we start." I took a deep breathe. I wasn't as excited as I thought I would be- that's why Abba God had my grandma drop me off. He was that excited about my first day too. I thanked Him, as I made my way up the staircase.

Staircases give you time to think. I knew one side of my family was more into education than the others. I found myself on the other side- people mostly worked on this end. I realized that people had a problem finishing in my family. I furrowed my eyebrows at this realization, and Abba God glanced over at me.

I was going to be the one to finish. What exactly, I didn't know where because people well- didn't finish. At least I had a general idea, and I knew school was one of them. People would start, attend a few classes but no one finished. Maybe, no one knew how to finish? Maybe no one understood how to get to the path so that way you're able to finish.

But what scared me more than not finishing? Being stuck. That was the moment, that it really hit me.

"Abba God, I'm different."

He didn't tell me the specifics in how I was different. But, we couldn't address me not being different any longer. That's the thing about switching environments- and getting into new spaces. At one point- I realized that's part of how Abba God has you to reach your full potential. One, by communicating even when it means by dropping hints. You're not made to flourish in every type of environment. That's the entire point of having a new environment- you learn about how you function and act in there too. This was my nudge. The- you're bigger than this one here.

I walked into my English class and ran into two familiar faces. Turns out, once they sat down to think about it the cost of college was stacking up. We all sat in the same area. I pulled out my laptop, and Abba God and I had our first day at college.

I can do what now?

"Abba God college is kind of a culture shock." You didn't have to raise your hand to go to the bathroom. You can get up, and leave and the professor doesn't even flinch. There was the syllabus, if something moved they would say something. My professor checked to make sure that we could understand how it was organized.

We could.

And that was that.

There was not nearly as much structure as in high school. Suddenly, getting up at 8am on a weekday was physically taxing and it never had been before. Praise be unto Abba that I had an afternoon course. I might pop up earlier on campus in order to get work done, or just to pass extra time.

Abba and I's personal time was undergoing a change. I was making an effort to balance time with Him and Jay. Abba God was during the week, and Jay was on the weekends. I thought this was a great idea.

Later on, Abba God mentioned that His time was being taken up by somebody's son. Well then.

Here I was, trying to balance time between the creator of the universe and somebody's son. You know what that was? Romantic idolatry. I was putting somebody's the place that Abba God was trying to spend with me. This was something else that ran in the family, but we didn't know it. In fact, later on I learned that idolatry was a generational struggle for multiple people in my family. In fact, that was one of the reasons why people would stagnate.

I'll speak more on what Abba God would teach me about that later. Abba God wanted to speak to about bigger things. But I only gave Him a certain amount of room to speak. Limiting Abba God caused, limited the instructions and downloads that He wanted to give me for other things in my life. In the time I did give Him, he was able to speak as much as I was willing to listen. Sometimes, I'd lay back on my bed and ask Him questions. However, my bible reading wasn't as in depth. I had an app, and I would look into it on my bus commutes.

The best way to describe this were steps. Abba God knew what was on step 17, and what He had for me on step 17. But, here I was on step 3, not giving time to listen to the instructions to get to the higher levels. This is because I was becoming comfortable on this level. When I was becoming comfortable on this level, then that was less initiative to go higher. This is part of how people in my family got stuck- in the idolatry of a comfort zone.

How to deal with it? Grab yourself out of it. When it feel it coming up- I push and keep things going.

This left us to enter into another conversation- when folks are in idolatry, especially romantic you open yourself up to Jezebel. Now, Jezebel is a spirit that isn't confined to a gender. Women can carry the Jezebel spirit and move in manipulation and control. Men can harbor the Jezebel spirit, and we refer to them as narcissists. The thing with narcissists, is that they demand to be worshiped. That's what makes an idol and idol, they take the place that Abba God needs to have in your life. When you participate in this, what you're doing is trading time to worship and grow in God, in order to stagnate and invest that same time and energy into another human being. The result, stagnation. The things is, the movies and Hollywood make this seem like a great idea.

It isn't.

One thing- you see how the idols in life already had plans on how to take me out? They leveled up progressively- and went ahead and kept going.

It's part of the reason how you never really get to accomplish your dreams in their entirety. Time and energy are given to us in order to invest continuing forward in life. Took awhile for me to get there though. But, the Lord in His kindness gives us a covering here too. When you come back to Him, and I mean really come back to Him- He's a redeemer of time. He's so good- that the time that you lost, isn't even lost time. You'll still able to get all that He has for you, but you've just got to leave that behind first.

Which, when you think about it is more than fair.

Perhaps the most interesting part, was that I was still able to keep up with grades, but then something else came into the mix. I needed more income. I helped out with my great grandparents for a bit of pocket money. I did housework and home care for her, but it was time for me to enter into the job market. Abba God pointed someone out at the mall when I was praying to Him.

I walked over, and it was for a local store that was looking to hire holiday help. I exhaled, because that meant I wasn't going to be a minor anymore. That had been the biggest hurdle I kept running into. I smiled and thanked Abba God, and began a couple of weeks later.

Abba God and I never really talked about fashion, and this was the first time that I dealt with 'adult fashion'. Part of my job was styling clients, helping out with fittings and keeping the floor in order. It was a luxury brand. I didn't think that I fit- but Abbalet me know that this was training for later. I gave them my work schedule, but sometimes I would have to do late nights. My earth dad picked up once at midnight, and said he wasn't doing it anymore.

So- Abba God sat with me on the last bus. The drivers would wait, and Abba made sure that I got home safely. I'd pretend to talk to him on the phone when I walked back to the house. It hurt, but part of me didn't expect my father to cover me in this way. That's when Abba God went ahead and stepped in.

This was the time period where I was introduced to nerd conventions. It was a way to cut loose- my sister made my first outfit because she wanted us to have more quality time together. Though we shared a common space- we weren't spending as much time together. J also liked the things behind nerd conventions- anime. No one told me that this was feeding idolatry too.

Hmm.

In fact, the first convention was relatively calm. But, I had opened up a door for an event in the future to continue forward.

In the progression of time- I added the job to the mix, with school, and helping out my grandmother and seeing . I can see why we took one class this semester. It was God giving me a cover to adjust. Between that, and processing more of the realities of the current state of my father and I's relationship- I needed a minute.

Abba God sat with me and gave me ten.

The end of the semester was here fast. Abba God and I sat in the library, while I typed out my final paper. We were on a time crunch to say the least. This paper came with some strict guidelines. Late papers were a failed final.

That's right.

I ran to the printer, and grabbed the final stack. Abba God and I sped walked to the professors office. The professor wasn't there.

She didn't have a slot to drop off papers in her door either.

And, one stipulation was that that paper had to physically be in her hands in the next thirty minutes.

It was a predicament.

I asked Abba God what to do, and He simply said- stay right here.

So I hummed a song and tapped my foot. Until I heard footsteps coming down the hall. My professor had been looking for me too! All three of us smiled when that paper entered into my professors hands. They let me know to contact them if I needed anything. Abba God smiled as that was going to be a seed for later.

Christmas wasn't as hard as the first one. Abba and I sat listening to this movie that we would always watch. It was my father's favorite one. I went to J's and Mama J got me my first designer wallet.

I broke out crying.

I wasn't used to nice things and Abba told me that I fit it. He had designed me for luxury, but it was something that I was struggling to comprehend. The gold plating and leather exterior were so special. The color was a rich red- adult but ladylike at the same time. Mama J said that it reminded her of me. If I was wallet, I might look something like this. In that moment Abba God not only confirmed me, but planted another seed. I was built for much more than I could realize at the moment. He knew it was going to take time for me to see that. In that in between time He covered me.

J asked me how the semester went and I let him know the updates. J's reaction was not what I expected, in fact his answer caught me off guard.

"It must be hard being perfect."

Abba God didn't talk to me like that. J said he was joking, but it didn't feel like he was joking. It was at this moment, I realized that there was a possibility of Mama J and I being close was the threat to J. Abba God glanced over to me, and looked back over to him.

That was a hint.

Another hint, was the fact that the comment he made hurt.

I dismissed it as a joke, but it didn't sit well with me at all.

Things were beginning to happen on the home front as well.

When I told my grandmother the news, I added that soon I was going to be able to help out with the bill. Or be able to cover it on my own. Really, I would just move to relying on Abba God in that area. That day something in my grandmother flickered.

I raised an eyebrow. Abba God told me to take note, what He had in me- was going to agitate what the enemy had in other people. That included those that I was close too. Sometimes, the enemies greatest weapon that the enemy can try to use are those closest to you. At this time, I didn't understand but what was happening was this. The enemy had spirits and what not running in my lineage that resided in the family members that I had. They were in other people too-that means that this was something I would have to learn how to keep in perspective. That's the fine print of being a generational curse breaker- the enemy will throw anything he can think of to get you to stop.

But Abba God is with you.

You have the Blood of the Lamb, which is more than enough.

When you know that- you're covered. And when you know you're covered, and who covers you- you keep going.

I'm not saying that it won't hurt. Some days you're going to have to tell heaviness and depression they can't have you. Others, you're going to be sitting by yourself after a fresh cry-calling out to God while you make new snot. But what I am saying, is that this is going to be worth it.

Y'all remember the David and Saul dynamic? No matter how David treated Saul, he still kept a level of respect because of the position in his life. This was my test, and honestly I failed this thing a couple of times. Later on, Abba taught me about other things that were made Saul possible to be Saul to David. We might talk about it here, or he'll have another topic in mind to discuss what was going on.

I laid on my bed looking at my ceiling again. That meant, that it was talk time with the Lord.

That realization was a hit in the chest. It was discouraging to say the least, and I had a fear come up. There were a couple of things that became apparent- the first, my father and I were not ready to repair our relationship. But, that didn't mean that my responsibilities for my relationship with my dad ceased. Neither did the instructions in the bible that fueled it.

Next, I realized how small I was in comparison to the task at hand. I knew what I didn't know, but I also knew there was even more I couldn't wrap my head around.

"Abba, I'll keep going. Please help me because I'm not sure I'm handling this well. I want to do a good job...but I don't know how to do a good job."

He smiled and reassured me that all was well. It had to be, cuz I didn't know how to do this without Him. That was a covering.

The next thing the Lord began to speak to me about was the spirit of poverty that was in the lineage. As time progressed, I knew more and more about poverty. The shocking part, poverty was much more complex than I had originally thought. I knew how to hustle. But, that was part of having a poverty mentality. There's a difference between hustling and investment.

The first step to addressing poverty, had to do with getting a financial understanding of reaping and sowing. Abba God had me begin to learn how to tithe. It shows Abba the level of importance that He has in your life. Physically, it didn't make sense.

We weren't looking at this physically. We needed to look at it from Abba God's perspective in the realm of the spirit. What was happening was this- the realm of the spirit had movement that we couldn't visually see. But every time that I took that ten percent- Abba would placed a seed in the realm of the spirit. Over time, it was going to grow into something amazing. Abba God has streets paved with gold, so why would he want us to be broke? That's quite an assumption. Besides, another things that keeps people in the cycle of poverty has to do with how you perceive receiving and spending money. Living check to check is a sign of poverty too- so you have to get to the root of the things to be able to see results.

Everyone was coming back from the first semester of college. I snuck out of the house to go to dinner and out ice skating. Abba God knew what was in my heart, and that was the fact that I was upset at missing out on my teen years. There was trauma there that He knew I wasn't equipped enough to process. Plus, I knew my father was going to have an opinion about me going out. Which, was infuriating and hurtful because he was being so selective about where to offer help. It was getting to the point where I didn't feel comfortable asking for his help if it was just going to lead to disappointment.

Even if I tried or didn't try, it was an equal critique. I didn't know how to respect someone that didn't respect or value me and it was hard. It took TIME to get that point of self restraint and I wasn't there yet.

Only the Lord knew how long that one was going to take. This is also part of the reason that He covered me in the in between time. There was a lot that He knew I didn't know. Abba God is kind indeed.

When I came back to the house, things didn't go the best. I went upstairs and laid down while looking at the ceiling. When I began to think about the upcoming semester, I began to get small again. I realized that there were more steps to this than my brain could come up with.

"Abba, how do I ensure I get all the steps?"

Walk with me and take it a day at a time.

It turns out I really like to organize things. I learned about 'writing a vision and making it plain' like in Habakkuk 2:2. My understanding of this concept was basic at the time. Due to my attention span, I knew things needed to be written down and organized. But later, Abba would speak to me about getting the concepts from the paper to real life. Especially, when it comes to the God sized things. That's a WHOLE process, and there's no way you'll ever be able to do this on your own. Abba and I sat, made a list- added some colors. There were a couple of things on the list. A job with higher pay because taxes were straining me- not my tithe.

"An important distinction," I said as I furrowed my eyebrows and continued to write. The Lord smiled. A scholarship, practice driving... I kept thinking and was bopping around to praise and worship music. That was the first vision board that I made for 2015. Now the one thing that I didn't do- was to double check with the Lord about the list itself.

8

The Concept of 'Next'

This was the biggest question that followed me around winter break. I didn't know what 'next' looked like.

Like, is it a square?

Circle?

Is it obvious?

Silent?

Demure?

Is there an arrow?

A flashing sign?

A neon light?

A shift in personality?

I didn't know what next looked like.

Abba God did. That's because He knew what 'next' was going to contain. It was going to contain new areas- places and spaces. That's part of how 'next' was dressed up- with different packaging. 'Next' was a vision board that I'd never seen before- nor could I make because I didn't actually know what was in there.

It didn't stop at the vision board, in fact it went beyond the vision board.

I was double coated up on a Tuesday morning, and struggling to be content with the process. Turns out, I was more of an end result kind of girl and stagnation and I were not friends. My headphones were playing another sermon when I went to hop on the bus. My curiosity was growing, much to the Lord's delight.

I had inquiries—not asks—because inquiries ask questions and seek answers. When you ask, you just sit until you get a response. But my brain needed to do some shifting. That included knowing that Abba God would give a response when Abba God wants to. His response will come in His timing, not your own. At the present, that wasn't too hard for me. I was more interested in conducting an investigation into the mind of the Lord. My brain and thoughts were shifting from the present to long-term investments, and the future that the Lord has for me. Abba had a big old grin and happy sparkles coming from His throne.

The meant keep going!

This semester was two courses. With the subject matter being a bit risque. I walked from my health course, chatting with Abba God.

"Abba, is my tolerance going to go up any time soon? I know I'm taking lighter courses and getting started, but I feel I'm stagnating." I made a sour face, "I don't like that."

Abba God began to walk beside me. That was Abba God teaching me about a capacity stretch. When I got this feeling, it meant I was going to be going up another level sometime soon. Abba God covered me here too, because OI- no one told me that learning how to sit during the stretch was the challenge in itself.

My patience during the stretch was getting an entire renovation. Which also meant, some areas were being brought to light.

Abba God had me getting uncomfortable with my major for a reason.

I sat in my psychology course with the realization- I wasn't about to be a psychology major. This course was based on some adult concepts, so I was getting exposed to an array of topics and information. Friendly reminder, to guard your gates. As interesting as this was- I missed science. Especially anatomy class, and this wasn't anatomy class.

Abba God told me to take note of this. He was bringing it up for a reason.

Noted.

Whew, y'all another area that was coming in hot had to do with time management. Abba God wanted His Him time. Of course.

Jay still wanted his time. School and work needed their time. Which had housework begin to enter in the self adjustment shuffling space. This meant, housework was fitting in where I could fit it in.

My father did not like that.

I took the time to explain to him one evening. I checked my breathing- I even checked with Abba God about what to say. I spoke with my dad, and asked that he was patient while I learned how to do the things. The bus added an hour to a fifteen minute car ride- and that made everything else a bit tough.

It went terribly.

I sank behind my door with a tear going down my face. Abba God's face shifted- with the realization that my earth dad couldn't comprehend the woman He created me to be. I wasn't going to be getting my earth dad's acceptance on this part of my walk with Abba God. This was when, I began to really resent my dad.

It came time for another convention. I did not conduct myself in the best manner at this one. Abba God had boundaries in place for a reason- and I didn't ask Him the reason why. Everyone seemed to have a reason to support what was going on outside of His Word. I was using this to fill the voids I had. Checking out to party for the weekend was one way to numb the pain I wasn't sure how to deal with.

It was during this period, Abba God was hard at work keeping me covered. I'm not saying my activities were acceptable, because they weren't. In fact, I opened myself up to dangerous things in the spirit. My mental sobriety was out of the window with every shot I took. The biggest thing, is that Abba God never went into the full amount of detail of all the things that He protected me from when I was in this phase. I think that's for good reason. We both know, if I had called on Him and applied the blood of Jesus then I wouldn't have gotten into this situation in the first place.

The enemy be schemin' and dressing it up as a fun time. When we know that's a whole lie and a half. It's hard to detect things when you're ignorant of knowing it exists. That's like 90 percent of satan's playbook.

Well my return from nerd vegas meant it was time to snap back into reality. It was study time, which meant that capacity increase also meant there was going to be an increase in new skills. It was time to hit another set of books!

Abba God and I were scrolling on the internet, and began to learn about savings and investments. I took notes, and sat to chat with Him about what was going on. This was a process to day the least, but a new one at that. This was another area that Abba God wanted to use me in. We also applied for a scholarship through school. Abba let me know that it was mine before I hit the submit button.

Now, there came a time where I was convinced I was ready to take it to the next step, to keep it in layman's terms. That was an awful idea to say the least. In fact, I placed myself into a precarious space by not applying boundaries.

I wasn't ready.

But, it was already gone- so I tried to justify all that had happened. It wasn't until later, I came to the realization that something had gone wrong. That was a process in itself.

9

It's Time to Math

Abba God and I had sat down, and I was speaking with Him about a couple of things. One, I had to take a math course. Abba covered me during that high school slip up- but now it was time to take the math course again. This time, it was going to cost money.

I prayed.

I had a new job, Abba God gave me favor and they hired me on the spot. That meant, this was the new place that I needed to be. The hours were generous during the semester. In the summer, they wanted me to do around thirty five hours. I thought that, and a math course wouldn't be that difficult to do.

You can re-read that last sentence to see where that went wrong. I thought it wouldn't be difficult. But I didn't pray about the course and the money and inquire about my capacity and balance to meet that. I should have, it would of saved me all sorts of time.

It was rough. Abba God was sure to cover me with a conversation that saved my community college career. And, that was the art of taking a 'W'.

Now a win, but a withdraw. It meant my GPA would remain intact, while we addressed the more pressing thing in the room. That was the fact, that I had gotten distracted. Working, school, and still distracted? When it comes to doing things outside of Him- yes.

A tear went down my cheek at work. It had been a couple of days since the 'W'- it didn't disqualify me from taking math again. It didn't hurt my GPA- but in this covering, the Lord was uncovering something else.

Pride and shame.

It turns out, I didn't ask the Lord if it was time to do this specific thing. That required a level of maturity that needed work. In fact, He covered me by making sure I didn't know this was an issue until we got here. It didn't mean what I did was right, but Abba God understood what I did not comprehend in the present moment. This was about discipline in Abba God's process for my life. It's important to know not to take steps ahead, you've got to ask the right questions to make sure you're moving in alignment. This was a covering. I needed to learn how to do this, but in the process of learning how- He covered me. It was hard to know about what I didn't know, and being vulnerable enough to be humble was difficult for me.

Another part was the professor. They went from 'you have all the potential!' to 'I guess I lied' when I went to ask for help. Apparently, help meant that I was inadequate now? I knew I was in my feels about that one.

I equated vulnerable meant that I could have a chance to get hurt, or worse dissapointed. You can flip back a couple of pages and see how that was a struggle for me. But, Abba God knew He was different. He wasn't going to let me down- but that was something that I needed to learn for myself. It was part of Abba

God's personality that I was going to need to learn about. This was a love based reality check, the reality being I needed to rely on Him much more than I knew how at the moment. It was a 'for the future' kind of thing.

But when Abba God said that we were going to math again in the fall, I almost slipped out the chair in the break room. We were going to go right back in it? What in the world do you mean?

He knew what He meant.

And I did too.

I was going to say something- and then Abba God shut me down with a simple statement.

Your pride shouldn't be attached to your self esteem. Besides, there was no need to be upset with the professor on this one. Was she wrong? Yes. Was I wrong for holding it against her? Also, a yes.

The first day of math, Abba sent confirmation of me being where I needed to be. This Professor introduced us to his cats. The girl that I sat next to had guinea pigs. We were good to go.

It was good that I first learned to drive in a Suburban. When you know how to drive that, any sized car is a breeze. Confidence building and patience were key- thankfully I went with the calm and seasoned family member.

In prayer one morning, I got hit with the notification. It's time to transition. The confirmation for that one was that sewage backed up through the floor at work. Did I know where I was going next? No. Did He? Yes. It was time to expand my gifts and talents. Apparently, I had a knack for beverages and drinks. It was fun, and at the end of the day I smelled like coffee beans.

The place Abba God sent me was a patisserie. Really, a french bakery. A talent of mine was to cook, and Abba God said I also knew how to bake. The cookies I made in middle school said otherwise. But He simply said it wasn't time yet for my baking skills to come out yet. Then I met Chef.

Chef was a classically trained pastry chef. The brain of chef intrigued me. I hadn't watched creative minds up close when it came to baking. I'd peer through the window, then Abba God gave me some courage to chat with him. I left the barista section and went to ask him questions. I didn't bother him on souflee day. But I would check in a little more frequently when he was making raspberry macaroons.

And if there was anything I had, it was a bunch of questions. Baking was closer to a science experiment than I had originally realized. But, the creative component to it was still a mystery to me.

This was- you guessed it- an introduction into the creative nature of Abba God. He glanced over to Chef and I chatting over mousse. Making note of the mental limitation I had placed on myself when it came to creativity and what I could complete. I didn't know it had been shaped over the years thorough various experiences. But Abba God knew the gift of creativity He put in me before I went to earth. Things were clogged up. The covering here was Him showing me, in small amounts what I was capable of in Him. But there was one thing He did give me, that I was aware of- an eye for detail. It was usually in the video games I'd play with interior design. But sometimes I'd help Chef with the decorations or picking colors.

Then one day, it hit me. Abba God sure put a lot of thought into creation. Earth and the heavens are a lot more complicated than a pastry. Plus, He made systems that are able to move independently but coordinate with others at the same time. Hmm.

That requires a lot more patience than being a pastry chef. Then, something else hit me- the face that I didn't know all the applicable places to be creative. I sat down.

Or maybe, the fact of the matter was I knew of places but I hadn't recognized them yet. I remembered that I used to like writing and poems when I was a little kid. Another hmm. Turns out, creativity is so creative it can go in a multitude of different spaces. Scribing, dancing, singing, painting, fashion design, pottery, scrapbooking, quilting, jewelry and who knows what else?

I've been in the box too long. And, as noted above sometimes it simply isn't time to execute an idea. You've got to skill build and learn, but that's part of the process you've got to be patient with too. Some folks can just pick sometime up and use it- for others it takes an amount of time.

Abba God put all this effort into making me a 'me'. It was time to talk about how I thought about myself, why, and how I showed that to the world around me. It was time to have other conversations about what made me, well 'me' as well. Yet to this day, I still prefer marscapone cream on a fruit tart.

It's luxury to me.

He came for my edges again. This time, with a question that rocked the entire world. The main thing here, had to do with the sheer fact that I was out here participating in activities to make humans- but concerned about it actually working.

This was the time where I first felt myself begin to outgrow J. I didn't want to acknowledge it in it's entirety. But Abba God was making some valid points. I knew He was right, but I wasn't sure how to go about things. Being with J was comfortable- even when we'd hit rough patches. It was better than letting go and being physically alone. If you didn't notice- this wasn't the healthiest relationship. You know what this means, Abba God was coming up with a way on how to get this through to me. He knew the state of both of our hearts, and I as farther away from Him than I knew. It was time to start coming back over. Yet, here I was filling His position in romantic idolatry with somebodies son.

I was on the way to campus, bundled up. That's when Abba God brought to my attention that J and I were growing at different paces. It was time for me to begin making a choice- either J or Abba God.

And I hesitated.

And Abba God sighed.

10

Wisdom

There were current mental patterns that I wasn't going to be able to take with me. Abba God had me making more room. This one was uncomfortable to say the least. The rewiring made it uncomfortable to sit still. Even standing up, running and walking around was important. That was because my current self, and the person Abba needed me to be for the next level were going head to head. As much as my flesh wanted to be held back, my spirit knew that wasn't going to be possible.

You're comparing.

I sat up and looked over at Him. What do you mean? Turns out, when you spend a lot of time on social media it's something that you end up subconsciously doing. And man, apparently that was something I did a lot. Instead of comparing myself to people, and where they were- I would look at statistics. Specifically, statistics concerning me and the obstacles that I had faced thus far. Abba God covered me here. That's because the chain that follows. One thing about Abba God, is that He knew the rooms He was going to take me in. Me minimizing myself, or being intimidated by those sent to help me was going to be of no help.

This was the time Abba God sent a phrase that I still reflect on today.

It's about being inspired, and not being intimidated. I needed a mental state that would allow me to keep growing, I couldn't afford to get stuck in a weird space. Progress can be a threat to those with a limited mindset. Plus, people were beginning to be intimidated by my own growth in Abba God. So this was something to think about continuing forward.

My guinea pigs were running around their cage playing a game of tag. Just then, something hit me out of nowhere. As much as I enjoyed reading proverbs in middle school, I hadn't formally asked for something.

It was the gift of wisdom. And yet, Abba God covered me all this time until I came to the mental space of me realizing the power of this question. Abba God describes wisdom as a principle thing in Proverbs 4:7 (KJV). Yet, I was out here without the principle thing. The Lord is Kind indeed.

Now, there were some things that I was hesitant on that became more of a can-do because of the applications of wisdom. Getting more involved on campus and making connections was a wise choice. Especially, when it came to spending more time with Abba God. I found a christian group on campus to check into during the week. There was a medical club to help network within STEM and make more connections there. Then, there was the realization of other wise areas to develop in order to steward my next. There was wisdom with school, my job, and navigating the following steps, classes, and my major, preparing for the future. As I walked in the beginning of wisdom, two things began to occur. The first- I was getting clever. The second, things around me were getting a bit smaller. I was outgrowing. But how do you outgrow things gracefully?

I asked where the resources were supposed to be coming from.

What a wild question to ask the Creator of the Universe, huh?

Money was a tool for expansion, not an end result. That's what I needed to think about to keep my focus on Him.

The wisdom in finances, for me realize that the summer course was necessary to sober me up. I thanked Him. He smiled.

Yes, Jay and I were still together. Yes, now I was getting dreams about things. And yes, the signs were pointing for us to separate. Yet, here I was with my stubborn self. It was time to reflect, yet I was adamant that those fractured, rose colored glasses still had some hold. For some reason, that was still more comforting than a blank face.

The interesting thing about this, was the fact that Abba God had designer frames in the corner waiting for me to put on. Better was there, but I was too close minded to realize that. That's something that I had to take accountability for when I was mature enough to do so. Even in that, the Lord was Kind enough to cover me until I got to that point too. In all actuality, looking back my treatment of Abba God was awful. Then comes the question, how often do we do this in our everyday lives?

When we hang out with what's familiar instead of going for what's best? Abba God in His kindness- still keeps His best for you, even when you don't know it's there. But He's also a respecter of freewill. This is why it's so important to ask Him about things. I've even found myself in situations, where if one person doesn't make a specific choice- that was the factor determining what Abba God was going to do after. Sometimes that meant He may have to shut a door Himself, or give grace until things got to a certain point. But at the end of the day, it was all going to work out for my good. This is why I wanted to be in the perfect will of God, and not in the permissive will of God later on. But that hadn't always been the case as you can see here.

What do you want to gain?

Satisfaction?

Ah, it's time to talk about control issues. For me, this popped up in areas of vengeance when people did me wrong. As much as we joke and meme about it- later on I learned why this was so serious.

God has His own feelings on matters such as these.

Romans 12:17 states recompense to no man evil for evil. Provide things honest in the sight of all men. (KJV)

Romans 12:19- Dearly beloved, avenge not yourselves, but rather give place unto wrath: for it is written, Vengeance is mine: I will repay, saith the Lord. (KJV)

And these verses reference back to Deuteronomy, which is slightly more hardcore. Not because the nature of God changed, but because this is the Old Testament. He seems more harsh, because we didn't have Jesus Christ as the final sin offering. Instead, there was a sacrificial system in place to being us back to that place of intimacy with Him. This is why I'm so thankful for the Blood of the Lamb. In all honesty, if this was the Old Testament, and we were under the old covenant. I wouldn't have made it. The Lord is Kind and covers us in that way as well.

The Love of God was still there in the same capacity, but the difference between the old covenants and the new covenant is the fact that we have the blood of Jesus. So God didn't change, the change in access to Him did. Just something to think about.

Deutronomy 32:25- To me belongeth vengence and recompence; their foot shall slide in due time: for the day of their calamity is at hand, and the things that shall come upon them make haste.

In layman's terms God has the knife. Not you. Yet, here I was gripping on the knife thinking that one jab wasn't going to hurt. In fact, it was going to be a relief. You know what was convincing me about that?

My flesh.

As if my flesh was going to be satisfied with a little vengeance. Flesh is never satisfied, that's why it rebels so hard when you walk in the spirit and cease from feeding it. But you know what the even bigger issue with this is?

One, wanting to take matters into your own hands is a sign that you don't trust God. Here I was, calling Him Abba God and still wanting to have control in this area of my life. That's when I learned, that all control really is- is not trusting God to be God.

Two, being petty wasn't going to help me. As much as I wanted to be petty, we simply couldn't do that. At this state, let me be honest and say shouldn't. It took a couple years and rounds of deliverance to get this out of me.

And three, if God can't take vengeance- that means that you're moving in revenge. Revenge is a form of idolatry. You're putting yourself in a position that God says belongs to Him. It's you placing yourself as an idol in place of the Lord. The Lord in His kindness covered me, while I got this out of my system. But that DID NOT excuse me from being in the wrong about this. The covering of the Lord is not agreement about your actions, it's about Him protecting His name. It's not about you, but your actions are what will impact what side of God you choose to fall on. Him giving us the option is a covering too.

We left neuroscience in my psychology course. I felt myself deflate.

A hint.

This meant a move was coming.

I didn't know the exact place or space of the move. But, based on previous conversation it was time.

It was time to become a STEM Major. Abba God took my science brain from my father, which was also the part that would have me forget things from time to time. Abba God reassured me, that I was built for this. Coming from the builder, you think it would be comforting. Instead, I sat for a second and began to focus on the things that may seem difficult. Working and STEM, when taking the bus was going to be a challenge. But, who was in my corner?

I snapped out of it.

But I was still snapped in with Jay.

Pride was in the way. Now, I know what we're all thinking-how can pride be in the way of a romantic relationship? The real question is what wounds or voids are the romantic relationships covering. It goes like this- the romantic relationship is the first section. The second section has a covering of pride. The third layer is the void that the enemy is using as a grappling point. The objective is not to have God enter into the void. If He enters in the void that means the person is healed, and the enemy won't have another holding center. It's a territory thing. If demons and spirits don't have bodies to inhabit, they run around in dry places looking for another spot. Personally, I don't see this as a 'me' issue, but a 'them' issue. I didn't rebel and get kicked out of heaven, that's a satan and his goonies thing. Yet, here they are- still victims.

Weird.

Now another part of STEM, the class prices increase. There's labs and lab books, other things you need to bring with you to lab class to participate. I sat and prayed to Abba God about what was going on. I was still keeping up with my tithes, although things were getting tight. I lost the bakery job too.

Did I handle this the best? No. I did not. I spent time on video games- which was another idolatry escape form. This was a theme that I needed to address, that's for sure. I had interview after interview, and nothing was sticking. That afternoon, I sat in prayer. I prayed. I knew I was going to be where He needed to be at the appropriate time. I trusted Him.

Abba God said it was time to apply to a program. It was an honors program, on top of the STEM course. They offered a scholarship, and even a summer travel course should I be accepted to it. We went to the interview.

Abba God covered me here too. When the confirmation came in I ran a lap.

Then the phone rang.

I made more at this job than I ever had before. I was going to be a barista again, this time with a more complex menu. Man, my husband must like drinks or something. It took time to get the skill set down. This was all for personal development, down to the cookie that I set on fire.

This was one of the times where Abba God brought my need to shift into new environments. One was forgetting the habits of the old environment. I didn't realize that they had automatic milk steamers that would turn off when you got to a specific point. At the bakery, we held it. I had the calluses as proof. So where at the bakery, this was no cause for alarm- I was taken aback when the trainer commented with alarm.

Ah, there are new things to take into consideration and shift into.

There were many new things going on. People were growing up, graduating, getting married. To know when it's time for a new thing is important.

I sat and thought about Jay.

Sigh.

11

The Not so Blindside and Going Outside

The holidays were over.

School was back in session.

This meant, the capacity stretch was in STEM, work, and an honors program. The great thing- Abba God made sure that the bill was situated!

Which also meant, that it we couldn't tap out. Tapping was not, and is not- an option.

J asked me about the semester. I told him.

He was 'supportive', but Abba God had me note what was going on.

Then came the blindside.

I wouldn't call it a complete blindside- instead it was more of a 'I was warning you in advance so that this wouldn't happen' kind of a thing. So- it wasn't a major shock to the system. Abba God, in His kindness- kept showing me the blind spot.

Repeatedly.

After an amount of time, the choo choo went ahead and came on down the track. That was the point of the warning- so that we wouldn't get to this point.

But no one told me about the blindside until later. But Abba God knew when it happened, and it was a covering that I didn't find out until later. At the time, this was one of the biggest moments in my academic career. It was important that I paid attention continuing forward to do what God accomplished me to do.

Now, Abba God gave another hint. See, now that I was getting into the academic swing- my grandma was looking to encourage the others to follow in my footsteps.

While the intention was good, there was something we needed to talk about. Abba God made us differently for a reason. A bear isn't a fish- because then it's unable to do bear things. And likewise, a fish is made to do fish things. I sat with her to explain this, and that when you compare a bear to a fish then they're able to be discouraged. She didn't realize this. Abba God gave her a covering until He sent me to lift it off of her. Now, things were different. She apologized to a sibling and they cried. We healed a little bit there.

I had to get orthopedics in my shoes this semester. Between work and all the walking, there was a lot going on. This was the first time that I felt the physical results of a capacity stretch- my fitness needed to increase as well.

J was quiet. Abba God gave J a covering, that was to make sure that he had the opportunity to tell the truth. Even when God knows what we've done- He still gives us the opportunity to come clean. That's grace. He gave me a covering too, because He didn't have it happen all at once. The group chat was...

Quiet.

Too Quiet.

I paused. Weird. That was a hint.

Then came the pictures of Him hanging out with a new girl in the group. I hadn't met her. My sibling did. That's when things came together.

I asked J.

He was quiet.

I kept pressing.

I asked him, if he had done what I think that he did.

He blew up.

"He said that he would tell you." I watched as my sister slinked forward.

One of the worst signs out there.

We won't get into detail, but we can say Abba God was right. I played myself. Later on I took accountability- but right now there were two things I wanted.

To be a victim.

And to get my lick back.

There was something I should have done, but didn't do. That was to grieve and heal. But that was also something, that I didn't know how to do. Instead, I suppressed and went for the jugular. Much, to Abba God's dismay. After all, He had definitely told me it was time to leave. Though I didn't deserve, in this He covered me too.

Because I absolutely ended up having to go up on pills. Classmates were concerned. Shoot, the Lord was like ??? Work, I retreated for a little while on breaks. My dad tried to call me lazy.

I snapped at him about how I can't compensate for everything that he can't do for me.

I was wrong for that.

He left me alone tho.

Now came the big test, when I was in pain- what was I going to reach for? I reached for things that didn't make reality hurt so much. The things was, pursuing any of these things outside of God- meant that I was giving the enemy the tools to continue to keep attacking me. It's like, the more you though you were progressing- you weren't. Kind of like, being on a conveyor belt and walking in the opposite direction. The progression wasn't there, instead you were stalling- or worse going backward into what you thought you were coming out of.

Abba God covered me, but brought it to my attention. A sibling ran into me keeping up with my chores in the kitchen. It took me time to be able to respond. They laughed.

My comfort was idolatry. I was reaching for anything, but the Lord to be able to fill a void.

J was blowing up my phone. No, I didn't outwardly break up with him. Arguably, we could categorize this as my first mistake. This mistake, I picked up. But I did tell him we needed to see other people. He already had a replacement lined up, so what was the problem? Now, I didn't realize it but I had become accustomed to not being enough. This left me with a low self-esteem and man, narcissists could sniff this thing out. That's right, I had more than a rough boyfriend on my hands.

The thing that had been sniffing out the lineage I was attached to- had found me. Abba God was doing more than trying to get me out of there- He was trying to protect me from getting re-snared by what other's had fought with. No one had one it yet.

Yet.

Then came the anger. At the fact that, no one really told me anything. Nor, had they stopped what was going on. That's why it important not to delay processing- and here I was at the same point that I had in the beginning.

Remember that professor I told you about?

He tried to try me. It started with a sharp comment on how everyone here came from a silver spoon. Oh boy. The thing was, this was a general comment- but he wanted to see who would respond. I tightened up.

I should have held my tongue. I simply said he should stop talking.

I poked the bear.

Next, was the comment about my daddy not paying my bills.

I said he would have, if I was a boy. Then I went on to give a synopsis of what I had been through in life. Ending with the question, "How much trauma until you tap out?"

I was not bothered for the rest of the semester.

I asked why this was necessary, the answer was- you're simply tougher than you think. You know how to preservere, and you're built for this.

I was cleaning again. As much as I didn't like doing the dishes- I needed to make sure that we made some quiet time during the day. Right when I started to be okay with being with Abba God and I.

You bet, J was ringing. Now, I change my phone number- and I should have back then. Then, I picked up and threw myself back into the area that I had just began to make progress to deliver from. It was to double check on the soul tie to see what was going on. I yelled at him. My dad asked me who I was on the phone with. I said my ex boyfriend. My earth dad went right up the stairs.

You know, the timing was funny. I gotten sponsored for a

summer study travel. The Lord said that it was mine. So- I proceeded. And woop! He confirmed His word for sure :) I was going-

Outside.

And I let J know, that we were technically seeing other people so He had no grounds to make those requests.

I finally checked back in with the people that I was related to. My grandmother had many opinions on what I had been up to. We had a little awards ceremony for the program. They were going on about the details and their favorite things about us during the academic year. It's funny because even as I type this, I needed a reminder myself. Look at God!

The professor said,

"There's something about you when you walk in a room, even sitting at your desk- it's the way you take up space."

Now, this was a BIG hint. Abba God was covering me in that, even thought I was going through something severe. I didn't look like it. Even when internally, I had a lot going on- my external look was that of power. Now, was it healthy power? Well, we can sit back and have that conversation later, I had a lot of healing that needed to be done at this point in my life.

But, that was part of what God needed me to do. To take up space. Even now, when I walk and I feel any way- I've got to be disciplined about how I take up space. It's HARD. But, the biggest thing for me to remember- is because Jesus Christ died on the cross, I have supernatural resources available to me from my Abba God in heaven. One, is the strength that's made perfect in my weakness (2 Corinthians 12:9). I lean in on Him more. But lately, He's been going for weaknesses that have been covered for years, and I'm having to re-learn how to yield. If you're in this space- I'm praying.

The other hint, was in relation to the resiliency and determination that the Lord gave me. It came in handy when facing opposition- because I know the God that I serve. That point in the semester, I realized I wasn't where I had been. But, I was excited knowing that I'm not where the Lord says that I'm to be going. We've got a journey. Arguably, this part of the journey was more comfortable than the first.

Now, while the Lord gave me a covering for the uncomfortable part- we needed to talk about something. That something- was how I dealt with being uncomfortable.

A hard-hitting conversation to say the least.

I sat with Him, and looked to the side. I wasn't ready to have it. Besides, when things were going well- they were going well. But the Lord wanted to address when things weren't going well. Or when I was so comfortable, that I spent less time with Him and moved on to other things. That part.

The summer study travel came up quick! It was lightweight on the coursework (for my professor, the others kids needed routine pep talks). Abba God covered me there too. I found a swing on the campus. We were in the hills of North Carolina in the summer time. I would go hear and chat with the Lord on the swing. I needed to still process and decompress.

Every person the Lord had me meet on that trip was strategic. It was incredible. Every comment and conversation did one of two things. The first- pulled me out of where I had been. Second- it was pulling me into where I was going with the Lord. The access to fresh ice cream eased the blow of the reactions to my current relationship status.

I wasn't single.

I wasn't together either.

And, that was the primary issue. Here the Creator of the universe was, watching me deal with somebody's son who wasn't even my actual boyfriend. Not like that was going to make much of a difference- rude is rude. Even in this, He still covered me.

Now, upon reading that last sentence you may have felt some conviction. Too often, this is something that we do to the Lord. Only recently, had He really brought up how ungrateful I'd been concerning Him. In a loving way, of course- but it still stung. He was right. And it wasn't until I came out of relationships, and was single- did I get that. He covered me, but this was one time where how He covered me made me want to be better. So, when I took walking with Jesus Christ and Him seriously, He was sure to cover the parts where I wasn't as mature as I needed to be. The Lord is Kind. Even when you're settling.

Phew.

It was around this time, I came across a modeling company. I know what you're thinking- girl don't you have enough going on? In the Lord's eyes no. In fact, He had built me for this. But I had to learn, how to build it. If there's one thing Abba God has down, it's how to make a system. A system so efficient in fact- that creation doesn't even have to think about the biological components of existing. We breathe and eat and hang out- all by His design. However, we do share this building nature with the Lord. We build smaller things, not so much a universe. We may be giving macaroni house- but even those areas of our lives come with two things. You need the resources, and you're gonna need a plan.

He knows we won't get it right on the first time. You might, or you may need a couple of rounds to keep going along and moving. He accounts for all the scenarios- and that's a covering too. We would overthink yourself into a circle- that's why the Lord says to give it to Him. He can handle it.

It was time to apply.

And figure out how in the world I could make this thing. Abba God stood by, really all I had to do was ask Him for the template. But my goodness there was work that needed to be done. But God knew that He's God- and He's more than able to do it.

My first exposure into the modeling world- wasn't sanctified. The jeans were high-waisted jeans, short shorts, and crop tops. Winter wasn't a deterrent. I was in deep. Abba God hadn't mentioned anything about my outfits- but then again I didn't ask Him. See- that pause tells you all that you need to know. Now, the Kingdom of Heaven HAS GOT to be the fashion center of the universe. You're telling me that the one who made jewels, couldn't adjust the physics of them to add them to an evening gown?

Can you imagine the manis? The suits? These things have to be out of this world. His creativity knows no bounds.

But at this moment, He knew that it was going to take time to add the capacity of what was going on. That meant, there was going to be an introduction to new things. But that also meant, that I was going to be different. You know how people can handle you when you come across as different. The Lord covered me when it came to this as well. There was still growing up I needed to do- because as much as I didn't want to be deterred by my feelings- I would.

I needed a backbone. Abba God knew it was going to take time to build the thing, and this thing in me. He is so kind.

12

How to Go About it

Abba God and I looked the pumpkin items. Fall was here! Which meant Abba and I were on our pre-semester midnight sign up extravaganza. Can't let all the good classes fly out the window can we? We clickety- clicked our way into a smooth semester. Ah, I sat back with my tension taming tea and took a sip. But not too much of a sip- the Lord didn't wire me for ingesting large amounts of catnip.

It was at this time, Abba God began to really hit the parts of me that were hindering my next level. In love- of course. But OW.

Sometimes the only thing that I could say was- "that was for me Lord".

Because it sure wasn't for anyone else. The correction of the Lord is a covering in itself. You don't correct people that you don't care about. Abba God was teaching me more about tithing, how it was watering areas of provision in the spirit. Now I didn't know the seeds that were there- Abba covered that because He wanted it to be a suprise. I'm sure He enjoyed me tilting that watering can in the spirit and practicing if I had the right aim.

"Am I doing it right, Lord?" Minimal splash was the goal.

You're doing great, sweetie.

I focused a bit harder.

The more I stayed at Abba's feet- the more provision came in! But that also brought something that to this day I still struggle with- and that's pride. Abba God taught me about fasting. Fasting sure is tough in the beginning. He covered me- in that when I would pick up something to eat and then spit it out I didn't get yelled at. He giggled when I would end up locking my favorite snack away to make sure that I wouldn't run into this predicament again.

The first day of Anatomy One two things were apparent. The first, Abba God was kind in me getting this professor. No wonder He was fighting for me so hard. When you had Professor Lia, you didn't want to go back. This was the second thing, Abba God KNEW how special He made Professor Lia. Which is why He had scooted us to be near each other, I needed to figure out how to navigate STEM. Not only that, but Abba God knew that I had need for an example.

The honors course was great, but He knew in my heart that it took a toll on me. I didn't realize it, but I needed someone that had been through what I was in. I didn't realize that I needed this, but the Lord in His kindness knew that I needed this covering. This was to assist the transition from my previous mind state to the next one. This, was going to done through the impartation of a pour.

After the first day, it became apparent that Professor Lia and I were going to get along great. She knew how to press and persevere, and the first day pep talk was inspiring. After this point, I opened up a bit more. I met the STEM starter pack- and began to branch outside of that. This was a point where Abba God did two things- He was introducing me to me. The parts of me that He knew were in there already. A new environment meant that there were going to be new hints.

Two- Abba God was introducing me to a new part of His character. The one where He sat back and decided to make neuroscience somewhere between plate tectonics and supernovas. He was teaching me the science part- that part.

I was spending less time on boys, and more time with Abba. Then, I back tracked. Even in that- the Lord covered me. There was a reason why He didn't want me mixed up- He was better than anybody's son. I needed to heal. When I healed- the voids wouldn't be so voidy. In fact, the voids wouldn't be voids- because they would be filled with Him.

But I didn't. In that, the Lord covered me too. It wasn't until later did I realize, He was also covering me in my ignorance of how He felt about the situation.

Long story short, I ended up in a situationship turned relationship. Abba covered me in this as well- but soon I was spending less time with Him. Again. Abba God knew how this could go, and the reason as to why this could go.

Midterms came up quickly. During the time period- the person I was seeing wanted to transfer schools. We'll refer to them as Enzo. They wanted to go nearby, but I didn't see the point in them staying close when they had better for them out there. If we were together, then we were together, if not- then not.

Part of the reason why things zoomed so much with this person- was because of a few things. I thought that they were what J wasn't, and they seemed closer to the Lord as well. But I didn't ask Abba God about this person's heart torwards me, or more importantly- how it was actually postured with Him. This is why I needed the covering of the Lord- I hadn't asked the right question to myself, or presented them before him. The Lord I was in the similar situation- it was just dressed up differently. This is why the Lord has boundaries, it's important that you don't overstep them. It's not safe- that's why the boundary is there. Asking for His perspective meant that is was important to inquire about what was happening. He has that aerial view for good reason. Abba God covered me when I fell back into romantic idolatry- not taking the time to heal put me back at square one.

And idolatry is the biggest hindrance to intimacy. You can't be intimate with someone you idolize. You can fall into other categories- but you won't reach the full intimacy the Lord has for you. Not with Him, or another person. That's an important thing to note for sure.

Abba God had another covering that I didn't know about until later. It was covering for a then friend that I came to realize did not have my best interests at heart. In fact, she was more jealous than I could comprehend at the time. The Lord knew that I needed this for later, but it wasn't time to reveal this yet. He knew I wasn't ready to handle all that came with it.- because that meant we would have to address all of the other problems in the room.

And guess who wasn't ready for that yet? This one right here.

13

The Community College Kid Hits the Middle

I was bundled up at the bus stop. Abba God's little marshmallow was back and in business. Enzo and I were long distance- so I would spend more time with Abba God during the week and weekends.

Now, one thing that was interesting for me to note was that I functioned much better in long distance relationships. It's like, Abba God was putting down supernatural safeguards to make a point. And- the point was indeed made.

I spent most of the time watching sermons and asking questions. The questions that I had depended on the day. Why were apples designed to look like that? What about colors, why red? Why did pineapples grow in bushes instead of trees? Was this a design thing? Or was it a function thing- or was it both?

Our personal time transformed. This was an even higher of covering than what I had known- that's because the intimate presence of the Lord was so strong. It was around this time, Abba God did a lil more uncovering. Peek a boo and what not. He began to show me more of Him. The more I got to know about His personality- the more I realized how inaccurate people's ideas of Him were. Genesis gives us the outline of what the original design for creation was. There was order, peace, and God was able to walk and be in relationship with Adam and Eve. Death wasn't in the picture. There was no struggle, lack or anything having to do with that. That's one of the most considerate and sweetest things that you can ever think of. I mean, we were designed to be intimate with Him and to live the abundant life forever- and it wasn't a hostage situation. His hospitality was, and is- off of the charts. As immeasureable as He is.

He already had Jesus planned. In the instance, satan and his goons came up in jealousy. When they were kicked out of heaven- they got knocked to the earth and hell. Hell was designed for demons. Just demons. But, they didn't like how hot it was- and didn't have the power to redecorate it. So they assumed, they were just gonna be given the earth. Quite a bold assumption isn't it?

So when creation came on the scene- the first thing that satan did was plot. The objective, how to have mankind give up their God given position so he could steal their things. The other motivation- to get back at God for holding him accountable for his actions. So when Adam and Eve sinned, things were knocked out of alignment. Yahweh still had mercy on them, and wanted to reconcile man back to Him. They tried a system to cover their new found sin nature. There was a lot to keep track of. Instead- Abba God put Himself into Jesus. Sent Jesus as His one and only son, to die as the ultimate sacrifice. This put Jesus as a mediator- not only is He the ultimate sacrifice- but He's able to mediate our human experience. It's complete. We're now able to be reconciled back to the Father and to be intimate with Him because of Jesus Christ. He is risen and seated at the Father's right hand. We see this in 1 Peter 3:22, which states, "(Jesus) Who has gone into heaven and is at the right hand of God, with angels, authorities and powers having been subjected to him". So, since He's got the sauce, we've got the sauce. As long as you've accepted Him as your Lord and Savior.

And here the enemy is tryna think you're not able to get what you've got. That's a whole lie.

While school was going, work was going too. I was being watched for a promotion at work. However, it didn't sit right with me. Abba God made a point here to mention that not every opportunity is a God opportunity. You have to ask if it's time yet. And, be sure to ask the intention behind the opportunity. And third, you've got to check and see that you're ready. For this one, I didn't feel like I was ready. That's because I wasn't. Declining that promotion was also a protection- turns out the manager dipped for a month. All the people that were in the position that I reported too were under stress. It was in the Lord's kindness, that I wasn't under stress as well. A new trainee and this? With all the other stuff? That's why it's important to check in with Him.

Abba God had me coming out of my shell this semester. It was time to get more involved. The more I spent with others, the more aware of how normal it felt to be alone. That was something that didn't need to be normal- nor should it continue to be normal. Ah. Got it.

This concept in itself was strange when you sat down to think about it- because this meant I wasn't use to having genuine human connection. That was going to have to go for the next steps that the Lord had for me. It wasn't going to be all at once, He knew this as He walked with me through it. I had to become accustomed to being in a bubble- outside of Him and romantic relationships and work you really couldn't find me much of anywhere.

Now, Abba was right there and eager to take time to comfort me while I went through the process. I'm going to be honest, I didn't know how to handle that at all. But He covered me in this too- taking it a step at a time while I became more comfortable with the idea of being uncomfortable. He knew that this wasn't the first time, or the only time- that I was going to need to have this conversation. To tell the truth- He was already aware of the multiple areas this was going to come up in. For now, this needed to be the main focus so we were really able to get things moving along.

The middle meant that there was something else that was upcoming. Abba God peaked my curiosity when it came to, well me. See, one day I came across a natural hair video. I'd never seen my hair before in it's natural state. Then, I became curious. What was the extent that you designed me?

There was discomfort that came with that comfort zone. He made a point by just coming to mind. I'd been getting chemicals to relax my texture for years, and never really thought about stopping to ask Him. Yet, He must have been a little offended with the fact that I hadn't made myself to be part cloud. When He took His time to make me into a cloud.

The realization hit.

That's when I went to hit the transition point. If we were gonna do this, we needed to go all in. At least, as much all in as I knew at the time. That's when my hair began to transition, and to be honest I began to transition too. Abba God had made His perfect timing on this one. That's because it was time to get to the firm foundation of things. Now, the methods about getting the firm foundation- those were yet to be seen or understood.

This was a hint and I got the clue on what the Lord was saying. It was time to learn about how He made me. He was patient as I learned how to detangle and moisturize the two textures. I would flinch when we hit the knots. Talk about an increase in patience. I was trying not to pull my hair out, I mean He knew the amount of hairs on my head. I was trying my best to keep the numbers as close as possible to the initial amount. Let's just say, there were new things that I needed to learn.

The more my hair grew, the more that I learned about myself. First and foremost- the beginning of the transition didn't seem so bad. In fact, it was pretty exciting. I heard that the more that you went along the process- then the more difficult it was going to be. Well, for now- Abba God and I weren't concerned right now. I was simply exited to begin the journey.

Then, came time to prepare to move to the big kid school. Time was passing quickly- so it was time to sit down and figure out what the next steps were. I rose from the floor with some notes, and wiped my eyes. Grateful that we were going to this part as well. It turns out there were guaranteed transfer programs that were available.

Oh okay.

I set a section aside to save money into. We were going to need books and what not. Abba God let me know that everything was going to be handled. I didn't know how- but then again I didn't need to know the full picture. I knew that He said it- so that means that it is what it is.

I sat and shuffled my papers, and Abba God rose with a smile on His face. My brain was beginning to think in terms of seeds and faith. This was new- I knew about tithing and being faithful in matters such as those. However- I had to come to the consensus that this next level was going to require an even bigger stretch of faith. I knew that this was true- and would continue to be true. So- it was important that I came to terms with this now. If I was going to be completely honest and transparent- I knew the steps for now. But Abba God was going to let me know the steps for later. This was a foundation that the Abba God was setting- something elementary for something incredible later on.

14

You're a (Bigger) Girl Now

My graduation cap had Psalm 112:7 on it.

She confidently trusts the Lord to care for her.

You know, when I was thinking about the graduation cap decorations- there were a couple of things that were coming to mind. However, I realized that like time- there were previous verses that had changed too. I needed a new one. A new version- a new place, a new space. Something to reflect where we were going, and where we had been. Then boom- this was going to be a perfect one.

Abba God sat with me while I was decorating. I wasn't usually into arts and crafts- but this was a different time. I shook my cap to make sure that all the decorations were on there properly.

We did a time jump.

My dad wasn't invited to my graduation. It turns out my earth dad was having trouble grasping who God was transitioning me to be. Things were beginning to feel small in some areas.

Abba God let me know that it was going to be a good thing indeed. It was a sign. I was growing at work too, and signing up for classes let me know that it was indeed time. I was not comfortable. Especially with the fact that I was going to need to get a car soon. I had the down payment, and was thanking God for the hoopty.

It turns out later, He knew that I was thinking far too small. He had something better for me. I didn't know this at the time- but a way that the Lord covered me was even when I thought small. Thinking smaller wasn't justification enough for me to lose what the Lord had for me. In fact, part of Him was astounded about how grateful I was for the small thing. And now, it was time for the big thing.

It turns out, this was something that I would grow in later. Being able to think about, and actually receive the God sized dream. Those types of things are important. Very important in fact. In fact re-examining those couple of sentences is humbling in itself.

The car showed up a couple of days before my first semester of (bigger) girl school.

She was not a hoopty.

Not at all.

She was beautiful.

Absolutely stunning.

In fact- all the times where the other go look and see's fell through weren't so bad anymore. And when I was crying on the floor a couple days prior wasn't so bad. Abba God knew that two hour bus ride was going to be rough.

The first day on campus began with a praise dance and a car scratch. Oi.

Abba God had everyone outlined that I needed to meet. I did another prayer while walking on the building sidewalk. The funniest part was the fact that we all had the same classes and the same class schedule. We couldn't miss each other if we tried. I found my spot in the library- which could switch into the spot for all of us if need be. There were resources and support that were different from my previous school. Including catering for club meetings- I asked the Lord to let me know when to leave my lunchbox at home.

Abba God covered me because at the moment- I didn't know the full assignment of why I was here. All I knew, was that I was here! I went back after class with a skip in my step and thanked the Lord for all that He was doing.

He smiled too.

Work was picking up too- I was speaking more into store organization and day to day operations. There were ideas that I had to help some problems in the store- and they were working out! So, that was all great.

My relationship with my family wasn't the best at the moment- I felt more isolated than I had previously been before. I didn't know what steps that I needed to take in order to navigate what was happening and what was going on. My dad and I were tense, I spoke to Abba God about it. Abba God let me know that at some point, I was going to have to go out and transition to a new space.

Um.

I peeked an eye open at the realization of what He just said. I just got a car note, and I was footing a portion of my tuition bill. Things were tight for the time being. But that meant, that He was about to expand into something else. But the big thing here- He may or may not give an announcement until you get right there. Ah yes, the trust exercise. Now this time it was a bit heavier- that comfort zone was being whittled away bit by bit.

To God be the Glory because we got to the breaking point. The point. The point where I you have to be honest about if you have to go another amount then you're gonna cave in. Now, this part is tough. But- once we did hit it- and I was STUBBORN about admitting it with my then proud self- relief came.

The rest of the bill was paid in full. And, it was coming again next semester. Turns out, the rest of the big girl school was going to be a full ride.

I ugly cried and made new snot.

You know how it is.

He brought the friends in. The study buddies. He was there for the late night study sessions where I would stay in the library until midnight. He heard the bags of Cheeze-its crinkling in the study room at night.

He also was there when I would visit the food pantry. When I thanked Him that I could drive a car back to the place I was renting. It didn't bother me much, I knew what needed to be done and what needed to be completed. This was for the end result. The part where things were going to make sense later on down the road. This was the sacrifice I needed to make now, so that things would be put together for later. Abba God looked down with a smile on every sacrifice. In the realm of academics and finances- I got it. But that wasn't the space He wanted this focus to go.

It turns out, that was part of the covering- because even in this I wasn't operating at my full potential. That's because the productivity and focus I knew- verses the level that God had already put inside of me were different. I didn't know this at the time.

But, that didn't change Abba God's mind- we had to practice this so once it was time to run I would know how to.

I was going to be a bigger girl later on down the road. But the interesting thing about this is- He was still covering me. Did I ask about how big He wanted me to get? Did I ask Him about the reference point.

This next section is going to be a shortened version of the events. We've got to focus on the Him part. Here's all the stuff that He was being Him.

15

The 'No' Event.

"NO."

Never in my entire life, had I heard the Lord speak to me in such a tone. My voice dropped to the bottom of my stomach. I faltered, my forward momentum supernaturally rewired for me to be knocked back. I grabbed a hold of the girl next to me for a quick moment.

I can't recall her name. I know my fingers were still hesitating in the air. My eyes watered up a bit. Her fingers didn't have a chance to hit send. I watched as the figures in black grabbed a hold of either side of her. Then she went farther down the hall, against her will. You could tell by how she was fighting back.

I called out for her. Abba God, I think He took her name from my mind. I can't remember it. But- once she hit the back doors I heard her scream.

This was, and remains the most pivotal moment in my entire life.

Out of all the times in my life. Our of all the times where I didn't know I needed to be covered. This was the biggest one. I'd like to think that I deserved it- but I didn't. I knew I didn't. That's something that I wrestled with for such a long time. Later, I learned that what kept me was a lack of fear. I knew Abba God. I knew some scriptures- but most importantly what I had was trust.

There's something about when a toddler comes to greet you. The waddle, the incomplete sentences. The pauses. The movements, the giggles. Abba God made the biggest move that day- and while He's love. And care, and full of mercy, truth and grace- something else prompted Him that day to ensure my safety. What ensures Him to remember keeping me safe. One His name sake- and two, the childlike faith of that little girl let Him. The one that's so trusting and full of love fear has no way of even existing. That kind of love.

I would love to reiterate a point- that this is indeed a work of fiction. I'll put that joint in Jesus name.

Abba God, why me?

I asked Him this on more than one occasion. Through laughter, through silence, through tears. Even when I couldn't ask- He would watch it arise in my heart. Even when He would help me to swing back to Him. Through the trauma, hurt and pain- that we tried to fracture that childlike faith that we both came to cherish so much.

As much as I went through, there was something that didn't come to my attention. And- that's the impact that this had on me.

On what was in me.

See- trauma is one of the greatest weapons the enemy has- which is still nothing for the blood of Jesus. But I learned that despite what was going on- I had to let Him move in so He could remove it. But even worse, it made it hard to be safe with Him. The goal was to fracture that childlike faith so that it couldn't function. But despite anything in life- though at times I did float away- He would always come get me. Or at least, be waiting close by while I was off doing things I wasn't supposed to. Which, at times I couldn't comprehend how bad it was.

The biggest challenge in all of this simply had to do with process. 'Simply' in the way the Abba God describes for Him. He's got so many things going around at any given time- who even knows!

But for me- this was not simple. In fact, it was hard. I had to learn how difficult I could actually be at any given time. There were parts of myself I hadn't met yet- and things that anxiety had shoved into suppression so I didn't know them for years. This left me with 500 panic buttons. Yet, the ability to somehow remain calm in high stress situations.

He- though slightly concerned at that fact- covered me there too. At that point, sometimes I was the weapon against myself. I didn't do it on purpose- but by accident. You know how it's like when you teach little kids how to cook! They bust the kitchen up. They're not too proud about it either- but that's the point. You have to teach them how to clean up their mess.

I'd cracked more than a couple of eggs, and managed to knock the entire container of flour off the counter. I grabbed a wrong measuring cup, overfilled the cooking oil. Left the water running. Broke a bowl. Then bumped the counter trying to pick it back up- which knocked the utensils to the floor. But the good thing is though it took time, I went back to learn how to wipe up the spills. To put the dishes back in the cabinets. The worst part- I was more focused on the cake so the process got bogged up. Much to the Lord's display, but those moments where I would stop and pause to clean or inquire- it meant that there was going to be more and growth.

But, my heart. That was another matter. First, how in the world did I have so much flesh that was something I needed to work on. The second, was keeping a soft heart while focusing and learning through trauma that kept piling up and wouldn't cease. I couldn't flinch. I couldn't pause. So I kept going.

You know, if I'm going to be honest. There was a reason that the Lord didn't bring up how bad this was. One, as much as this was a defense mechanism- we needed to ask a real question. If He was allowing me to use this as a cover, what was the reason? It turns out I was not emotionally equipped at the moment to process the actual trauma I had.

As you go through life there are something that you're sub-conscious won't give you the ability to process. That's because you can run the risk of having a mental or emotional breakdown if too much hits you all as once. The defense mechaism, was a blessing at this point in my life. Thankfully, Abba God had me to begin processing old trauma even if new trauma was coming in.

I chatted with some therapists. We started with the past stuff- and everything was completely fine. We'd talk- get to my mom and dad's stuff then move to the more recent. We had a conversation about past boyfriends. My taste was awful, and to be honest when you've had two back to back and they end just about the same- you're the problem. In fact, Abba God had been waiting to bring this to my attention. At the end of the day, they were as faithful to me as I had been to Him. And He sure didn't say anything when I was fornicating, but I sure vented about being a victim with how it all went down.

Oh.

There was one therapist that I had. It was going like all the rest of them. Then we got to the divorce and I skipped to the next part.

Her eyebrows rose.

Hmm?

"No slow down. We need to talk about that part."

"What part?"

"That part. What happened when your parents got divorced?"

"You mean...?" This caught me off guard.

"What was the bad period?"

No one had ever asked me that before. It was in good reason- that was because when I did talk about it my body responded. My eyes watered up. I didn't realize until a tear fell. God uncovered this one at a slow pace, I felt the first layer. Then the second. The third.

It wasn't until I got to that point. My therapy went in layers. Most recent trauma, then we'd work our way back. At first, I was infuriated at the amount of money spent before we got to this section. Then, it came to my attention at the simple fact that- at that time I wasn't ready.

But that didn't give me an excuse not begin the process.

Abba God knew that process and I didn't necessarily get along. I would support everyone else but me. As much as I thought it was positive- He knew it wasn't. But- I had to be ready to receive the that this was a problem, and it needed to be addressed. Y'all know how hard it is to hear with trauma ears. However, I am thankful because this was then something that I took into account with other people. Sometimes- they're just not ready yet and that's completely okay. It's an important thing to mediate on when someone's on the verge of crashing out.

It doesn't excuse the behavior, but you'd be surprised at how powerful a gentle response is when people are going through things. That could be the one thing that makes them rethink it all. Just a thought.

Abba God and I made the most progress when it came down to this one. If we're going to tell the truth-I went through more in these couple weeks than in the past couple of years. I hope and pray that everyone finds that one therapist where you know God is telling them about you. It's a powerful thing indeed. I couldn't even dodge my eyes past her to tell the truth. It's like I was sitting on a screen with Abba God situated on the other side.

I had to face things. Now, these things were not in relation to the 'No Event", but unraveling all the things that prevented me from getting to be me.

16

We're Breathing, Dude

We're going to fast forward for a second. To the part where I shouldn't be alive.

Which is this part- the one that I'm typing now.

You know- the most interesting part about being covered, is that you often don't understand the extent of your covering until later.

I thank God that doesn't exclude you from what happens when you go through it. The past couple of years had me facing a situation. Many times, a situation that others would deem impossible.

But nothing in impossible with God. That's on Luke 1:37. Now let me tell you- you don't know the extent of the possibilities of God until you run into an impossible situation. The thing is, when you approach situations you don't know if they're able to be impossible or not. Now things that are just restrained to earth are one thing- but how about when we throw in aincent evil groups that are trying to take you out because of things in your family lineage?

God covered me in the warm up.

The amount of times I should have died in my sleep, I lost count.

Drowning.

Fire.

Traps.

Snares.

Obstacle courses that dropped you off into the abyss.

Ostriches.

Death itself.

All the way up to surviving the hunger Games- and if I didn't pray for the dreams of others and myself that night we all would have been gone.

To say the enemy wanted me to die is one thing. But the sheer extent was eye opening. That isn't including the times that the Lord put His strong arm in the physical realm. He knew the car accidents, gang stalking rings, monitoring, traps and snares the enemy had laying around. Yet, they still persisted. But they didn't take into account that fact that God said I'm going to live.

For some, it registered as a suggestion- although I am unsure how that is the case. Abba God let me know that many who don't understand His sovereignty may do things such as this. It doesn't make Him any less of Himself though. Which makes them run themselves into the very traps that were set for me, because God is God.

Now, I later on realized that this is also part of a covering. One, my delayed reaction to registering fear in situations. But, that was the result of the gift of faith that the Lord had given me. Even if there was something that I did ask Him, it was something that was done in wisdom. And, He gave me wisdom- so when I sat down to think about it- this is all Him.

I inhaled and exhaled.

And every breathe testifies to the kindness and faithfulness of God.

If you thought the enemy was going to tap out after that, you're wrong. In fact, the enemy came back for the kneecaps. There were folks who got smooth played that criminal high key- which left a lot of the promises that I was waiting on- broken. Messy was an understatement. In fact- there was so much that went into the sabotage- the only thing that I could say was this.

God don't like ugly.

Now, as to why you would get more ugly idk.

I sat in my car. I had a couple of says worth of clothes on hand trying to figure out what to do. My bible was on my lap- and it was time to get the front on my car window so no one could peer in.

I had an address, but I didn't want to stay there. There was a bunch of trauma from that house. Abba God knew that's what was making it hard for me to stay there. The next part of my life depended on it- but He was going to send a revision because He saw what was going on behind closed doors.

He saw the nights I cried into my bible from the pain. How I sometimes felt that having clean hands and a pure heart wasn't too much avail. I didn't want to compare myself to the wicked. Especially when they wer flourishing despite my objections. God said, He was going to handle it. It was time to leave room for Him to move on my behalf.

So, I prayed.

And cried.

Abba God came to wipe my tears.

I sat with Him.

He sat with me.

We sat.

When I would try to make a move things weren't situated. There would be a bump. One night, Abba God let me know that I couldn't stay there that night. The people in the house were planning to kill me. Turns out, later on Abba God revelaed a network of those who were jealous of me that were trying to come up with a way to kill me. I got replaced, stepped on, run over, attempted to look like a liar.

I sat weeping and Abba God pointed out a page.

My clean hands and pure heart were not in vain.

I flipped a couple of more pages. There was the reminder that God was fighting for me, but I just needed to focus on myself and being still. It was hard to say the least. I didn't know how it be still. Someone actually withheld instructions for the next steps of what God had for me, and that's part of the reason why I was sleeping in my car. Abba God said it wasn't my fault because I wasn't told- that's not fair. The people on that level couldn't handle me. The rejection was protection for the next level. That's because no eye had seen, nor ear heard what He had for me.

I flipped another page in the bible, while Abba God was back at the drawing board. He's making a plan. Now there was also the realization that people hated me, and wanted to be me so much that there they wanted my dead body.

That one took some time. It's harder when it's people that you honor. Oi.

So- we were at the drawing board. Abba God and I were in building mode- there was so much that I needed to do. Especially when it came to learning how to stay focused on the task at hand. I needed to write.

I was a writer.

In a lot of different areas.

I needed to discipline myself to continue forward. That was the main problem. There were scriptures about it to. But I had to focus on getting those in my head- which was easy when I wasn't running around like a chicken. I was praying more than being a chicken to make sure I was sitting down. But sometimes- I needed to sit there and scream and cry about it.

Abba God let me know giving up wasn't an option. He put His foot in designing me for a reason- there was no reason to quit. He was with me! Which is what was the most important.

Nw I know we probably want the update. What's the squeeze! What's the details on what's going on?

Needless to say- we're still breathing and the enemy is trying to come at us with all but the kitchen sink. At this rate, there's so much that I've been through certain things faze me less. Abba God let me know that was part of my conditioning process- there were some soft parts of me that couldn't remain soft. But there were certain things that could only arise from me in certain situations. So at the end of the day I may have been on the verge of homelessness once more- but do you know what incredible thing came out of it? The fact that I learned how to focus.

Focusing isn't something we think about all the time (especially when you were me)- so we needed to take the time to undergo brain training. See when Abba God gives you something to focus on- you have the ability too. There's just a plethora of things that can be clogging your lens.

Turns out, some of the things that I struggled with in the past weren't all the way gone. That was the hindrance, me not Him. And yet, He still covered me through the learning process.

Through the pain.

Through the tears.

Through the years.

Through the 'yes' and the 'no' and the 'this really hurts'.

Through the people who you thought were in your corner but weren't.

To come to the realization that for so long I really didn't see me the way that God did. I let a lot of people treat me badly. I needed more boundaries. I needed to get better at saying the word 'no'. I needed to stand up to people that were trying to tell me otherwise, and remove them. There was a part of me that was scared of confrontation. I'll let you know right now- that part of me died.

I watched her go too.

The Lord covered me to get to this point. To the point where I underwent one of the biggest shifts of all time. Where it was what the Lord said about me or nothing. I didn't see opposition as opposition- I called it a distraction and moved forward. This was the focus. Focus past the distraction. Focus past the jealously. Focus past the coveteousness, clip comparison. And letting Abba God teach you where and how to aim. Turn out, there were some things I was so used to being familiar- I didn't realize how bad it was until I snapped out of it.

I found out something powerful. That God is indeed still God.

And, despite what was going on around me- my heart mattered. There were times when I didn't think that was so. Not at all.

Not when I heard the bullies. But I remembered my character requirements meant that I couldn't act out in my flesh.

I couldn't be offended. I couldn't have fear. I needed to learn how to love, and how to be love. How to function in love I hadn't known before, and then know the boundaries that were going to be necessary.

Because once I sat down and genuinely thought about it- no matter what happened to me I broke my heart too. Abba God covered me that entire time. Until that thought hit, and I felt myself shift into a next.

You've got to take your power back.

You've got dominion and authority.

You don't have to live in the aftermath of anyone's mistakes. I don't care how big or how small. Is God not God? Is there anything that is impossible for Him?

No.

Exactly.

He reminded me to be bold and courageous, but this didn't make sense for me until about now. My bold and my courageous depended on the category that I faced. It was going to show up differently to navigate and accommodate challenges that the Lord hadn't seen coming. But He covered me again with this phrase, '...while still knowing how to be love.'

Who in the world has the template for that?

No one.

That's why He made me. See the me that Abba knew included some things that were wrapped and stuffed under past- and to be frank- even new waves and levels of trauma. Because of this there was going to be another section we needed to talk about.

It helped when I read scripture. Even more when I could recite and apply it. More when I had those moments where I laid on the floor and got it all out.

Then there were the moments where you wonder, "Dang Lord how hard did you go when you made me", and you get a smile. There's more that needs to be done or to be complete continuing forward. I had to understand that empathy was a superpower- but only when you use it correctly.

No where in the Bible does it state that love is gullible.

Neither does it mention having a lack of boundaries.

Neither does it mention watching people destroy themselves because you wanted to shield them from the consequences of their actions. Love doesn't block sowing and reaping, love knows that God knows what needs to be done and what they need to learn.

Love lets God discipline.

Love knows when to move forward and when to stay back because love matures. Even in uncomfortable circumstances.

So all of this to say one thing- The Lord in His kindness, covered me with His love.

That's incredible to say the least.

And I'll keep saying it.

The Lord is Kind.

He's going to continue to be Kind.

And He's going to continue to be mine.

He's not done with me yet, in fact this next chapter is going to be full of the biggest plot twists of all time. For no eyes have seen, nor ear heard the plans that the Lord has for those who are called according to His purpose.

That's the fun part.

We've got even more secrets to keep now.

And He's made sure that no matter what the enemy tries to do this time- I cannot be stopped. He's in me. I will walk in the fullness of all He's called me to be, in fact- so much so that He's already got it handled.

Set it in stone, and tuck it away someplace secret. For I will live and not die to declare the works of the Lord. I will bless the Lord- all my soul and all that is within me. I will bless His holy name and forget not His benefits. I've already overcome the enemy by the blood of the Lamb and by the Word of my testimony. It's already been situated.

And know, that the Lord will continue to be kind to you too. If there's one thing that I thank Him for it's the sheer fact that He is who He said He is. And- that's He's going to be who He says He's going to be. This brought up questions about my own consistency- emotionally. How, when, where and why would I show up- or would I continue to show up. If there was going to be a need for me to continue to keep showing up- would that be a reflection of my inconsistency? Or is that being responsible with my emotions? I knew I still had the personal responsibility to walk in love.

This was where I found myself going in circles for a long time. This meant that there was going to be another portion or place that Abba God needed to speak to me about. But this was going to be a new place and section that needed to be addressed.

17

You're not Done Yet.

Now, if I told you I was writing this in a comfortable space or position- I would have been lying. In this season, Abba God was going to change His approach. Now, all things are possible with God. He was having a standoff with that and my self perception. Now I know what you're thinking- how in the world was He going about it?

It's giving the book of Ezekiel and a dry bones situation. At first, I looked at what was available with anger. Frustration. I was asking Him- you want me to go from this- to THIS? with

Points to air- this.

And to my dismay, the Lord simply smiled and said "Yes."

It was a standoff. Realistically He could have just smacked me around with a brick and told me to sit down. But He didn't, because this meant one thing.

That the me that was in there was about to completely bust forth. And it was going to be all He had made me to be. That was His excitement, along with the fact that I was going to get to know Jehovah Jireh in a completely different way than what was known before.

But the problem- and it took time to realize this, was the fact that the problem was me. I was my own standoff- my mental states and strongholds were havign a verses battle that had never been seen before.

See- Abba God is Alpha and Omega. The beginning and the end. He's the creator of the universe. That means all the things-yeah, He knows about all of that too. But I wasn't allowing Him to show Himself. Because I didn't know how to allow myself to be able for Him to show Himself.

Being the gentlemen that He is- He isn't going to cross over into other areas and territories that He isn't welcome. That includes the realm of your mind. There were some subconscious processes and thoughts that I needed to address. We got to the quiet ones. The super silent ones that came in before I knew how to remember anything. That level of trauma. That level of difficulty. The demons and spirits sitting in me that had so much rank it was absolutely ridiculous. Those.

The thing is- it all happened through a simple conversation. A moment of quiet between He and I. The silence when my brain began to click and I came to the realization. The reason why my pouting and comparison and waiting to be comfortable to build wasn't going to do anything.

I had the opportunity to build when I was comfortable.

And I didn't do everything that I was supposed to.

That's because that idolatry of comfort was in the way. So that got knocked back a couple of pegs.

Because the thing was, I didn't need external comfort. Or external validation. I needed to get out of the comfort level that people pleasing left behind. The one that paralyzed my ability to rely on God as God. The one what was adjusted and accustom to needing to feel comfortable or some form of comfort to move. This was the residue of idolatry that it turns out had been built up in me as a child. The same mindset that was getting in the way of God being able to be God.

The ant.

The ant in the book of Proverbs- He builds. He continues building. No one tells Him to build. In fact, they can't go to the ant store. They don't do ant delivery. They don't. Yet, here I was complaining that I didn't have the finances to build this things. I'll tell you what I sounded like when that realization hit- like a complete brat. It was awful.

The ant didn't take the time to sass Jehovah. The ant knew what was inside of it. The ant knew his potential. He knew the abilities and talents that Abba God put inside of Him. He knew he was built for this, and He knew that Abba God had everything he needed to succeed- whether that was internal of external.

That's when I realized- it hadn't been about lack. Abba God wasn't decreasing what I had to be cruel. At times it felt like it, but I knew that wasn't His character. Which made things more interesting- because at that point I knew that part of me was the problem.

So.

I sat there. I looked around and took a breath. I realized we were hitting the final levels of what was in the way. I had beat the snot out of satan. It wasn't anyone in his camp bothering me. It was me. This was the residue of me from the other things that I had been through. This was the part where I was facing me. At this point I was my biggest obstacle.

That was the moment that I decided I wasn't going to be an obstacle to myself anymore. I pulled down that stronghold, and let God come in. There was no boundary, or barrier- anymore. I realized that in Him is all that I needed, and would need. That I am equipped for this good work, and I needed to understand that before the provision came. The ant needed to decide the plan of action before he went forward. A plan where he assessed himself. What he knew, and even what he didn't know. But- he still made sure to continue forward to be all that God called him to be. He made sure that he took care of himself, and once he knew that he reached out to the community.

I needed to be better with my pour and personal time.

Don't know if ants have bible study, but I imagine they check in with God from day to day. See, it's not about the career, the car, the place, the things- it's about seeking first the Kingdom of God. It took me decades of my life to be able to conceptualize what that means.

The Kingdom of God is internal as well.

The Kingdom of God includes your gifts and talents.

The Kingdom of God includes your build.

The Kingdom of God is external.

The Kingdom of God is reflected in the physical resources that are on the Earth.

The Kingdom of God is spending time to take care of yourself.

The Kingdom of God is pouring into others to help them be all that God has called them to be as well.

The Kingdom of God is more complicated- and more beautiful than you could think of imagine. But more than that- things are incredibly simple.

Sluggards can't be sluggards until they understand the Kingdom of God.

That's when they turn into an ant.

But you know what's even wilder about the ant? It's the fact that the ant doesn't even know all of that at one time. In fact- the ant isn't able to think that far ahead. But, it doesn't have to. Instead it's able to become all of those other things because of one thing. And that one thing- is the fact the the ant just follows it's sense of smell. It's God- given sense of smell. That's what it's relying on to tell it how to build- so there's something more powerful than everything that was just mentioned.

It's trust.

Trust in God.

That's the power of the ant- the fact that the ant knows what it can use to navigate. And that navigation system when you sit down and think about it is God Himself. And that's more than enough.

So then came the conversation- what's in the way of me being an ant.

Well the answer, was me.

There were parts of me that needed to die, and began the process of dying and needed to continue to die so we could move forward. See- this level of me (even with all I had undergone) was not going to be enough to go to the next level. That's the thing. I had to be an ant in this season. This meant, that I was going to get to know God in ways that I hadn't thought were possible before. That doesn't come with comfort. Because the thing is, I was always going to be 'becoming'- because there were parts and versions of me that existed that didn't at the time. So when some would come, others would have to drop and fall off. Capacity would would would have to increase. And that process was hard, especially when pride would try to pop up. Not to be proud- but to try and set a guard or shield from the pain that I was feeling. It was like a defense mechanism, and that was something new that I hadn't fully realized until now.

That's because now was the appointed time to see and reveal the thing. Wow.

So this meant that the Lord took you on the scenic route? No.

In fact, this was more of a juice press and I was the orange. He knew I needed a deep reset, and I had to continue going to yield into the process. This meant one thing- I had to get my tolerance up. I couldn't be ready to bend and break and have issues/ problems at the slightest. I had to focus. So Abba God took the time to get me to focus. At the end of the day, the enemy doesn't have to do much to oppose you when you're unfocused. Now, it's learning how to focus in that environment which is the most difficult.

At first, I complained. Abba God sat with me, patient until I understood why this was going to be necessary. That's because next level me couldn't be distracted by this level stuff. I couldn't tap out because things were 'hard'. I needed to go ahead and choose my hard- but more than that I had to continue to focus no matter the hard.

Was it fair?

At the time it didn't feel like it. You're telling me I almost died six times this week- and that's no excuse from me typing another chapter? I was offended for five seconds- and that's too long? I wanted to cry and grieve- but I've got to pick myself up faster? I had to discipline my emotions. The craziest part is- Abba God and I never spoke about being emotional. If anything, I hadn't learned how to process emotions because I had not been that open to speak about them. That was a hard thing. But now, I had to learn how to speak about them, process and move on? Level One was HARD.

Abba God then spoke to me about producing even when I was lacking seed of finances. I would sow- and hit bumps but that didn't excuse me from pausing from being able to sow. No.

Abba God had a specific set of lists and circumstances that I needed to work on and follow. It meant, I had to grow up in ways that I didn't think were possible. Even when people looked on in jest. That couldn't overwhelm me either. Or tempt me to quit.

In fact, when it came down to it- I understood something. Abba God smiled when I came to the realization- that me thinking that way was a remnant of comparison too. Oi. They can get away with this- and I can't- that mentality had to go for me to do this thing.

I cried about it.

Abba God simply reminded me that I have no successful enemies- and he contends with those who contend with me. But He also re-aligned me on how to conduct myself during the 'get backs'. When their reaping came- I couldn't act any way that I wanted to. I couldn't jest, or jeer. Because He would turn Himself around and come right back here over to me.

Abba God and I chatted about the other things that I would do instead when the time came. One of the best things that He's able to provide is for you to go someplace else for a little bit. And if we're going to be honest, that's completely fair too. There's a whole lot of power in minding your business- especially when it comes time to give an account. Abba God pointed out that minding your business also means that you mind your square even when there's fires going on in other places. That's something else that I have to make note of as well. If we're going to be honest- at the time- it was a major area of improvement. But- we got it now!

See- that counted and counts as me watching where I pour as well. It was time for me to put God first in ways that I hadn't fully understood or know about. The strongholds and old patterns were coming down something fierce. This meant- there was going to be a new me. A new me that God knew already- but one that others hadn't seen before. In fact- this meant God was going to be smiling as an audience of one for a lot of things in life. But that meant we would be smiling together- and that meant the people pleasing and comparison had to go. There's no way that we would be able to come back to where we were.

Honestly even as I type this- I don't want to go back to the shell shocked version of me. I like the one that's more like who God made before. Abba God- I like what I'm becoming because it's who I've been in you.

18

A Marvel in the making

HAHAHAH GET IT.

"God, thank you for the grace of today. Thank you for the grace to get things done." I exhaled. The sun shone on my face- a good morning from heaven. I smiled, and sat.

This part is ongoing at the moment. This part is uncomfortable to say the least. In fact- this part was the part where the Lord sat me down with my flesh. There were areas in my life that needed some work. He knew this- but the enemy knew this as well. So- there were snares.

The worst part was that technically- this part came down to me. It was tough to say the least. I had to be honest with me about me, and why I was the reason that some things weren't moving along. Now when it comes to levels of trust- I also found that there were some people I was having issues trusting again. However, it became apparent that some around me that wanted to help- did not want to help. I mean- they didn't want to give healthy help. It was the kind of help that they use against you sometime later.

I found that there was a plethora of things that I was going to need to let go off. Cars, people places and things. In part- I didn't have the boundaries at the time to rid of certain things or to call stuff out. But, now I did. Thankfully- I wasn't going to die because of this. As much as the devil was sitting down and slamming his head against the wall- nothing was going to be able to prosper. I had to get out of the 'woe is me', 'this is hard' to it doesn't even matter what it is- we're trucking through it because greater is He who is in me than he who is in the world.

Now, I also had to think that the folks that were betting on me to not make it were about to be in hot water. Well, they were in hot water. Arguably- if I'd taken the time to call them out when it was smaller it wouldn't have gotten this big. But then again no one side was a victim.

One of the biggest things I realized is how detrimental wanting to be a victim in any situation can be. That's because of a couple of things- the first you have the power and self control to do, or even not to do something. That's going to be an important thing to know about going forward. Secondly, being a victim is a sure fire way to shoot yourself in the foot. Especially, when you've made a wager that you know you're not going to be able to pay. I began to wonder about the mentality necessary to do something like that- and I came to realize that people genuinely assumed that death was a sure fire way to avoid accountability.

It's not.

In fact, someone remaining alive when you tried to kill them doesn't make you a victim. I can't say that it makes you a fool either because at the end of the day- if you call people that you're in danger of the fires of hell. So I won't say that either. But what I am able to say is this- there are so many reasons why the Lord sets boudaries. Often- it's to avoid worse case scenarios or snares. But because the fact that wasn't explained it doesn't make you the victim. In fact, even in those types of situations you have the power to make a different choice.

Unless you've sold your soul or something-if you have you may need to think less on coercion and more on kindness because you're butts on the line. Plus when you think about it, you've got some big bets and no dominion or authority to take it back or break yourself out. Talk about white knuckes. But then again, God says that thou shalt not kill. So that was the boundary. If all it takes is prayer, and someone knowing bible scripture without fear to take you out- then why sell??????

Like ??????????

No situation is ever impossible, because everything is possible with God. At the end of the day, wouldn't this bite you in the butt more than the other party? In fact, at the end of the day I sat with this as I was typing.

See the thing with being a marvel in the making, is the sheer fact that it ain't gonna be easy. That's because of the above statement, you need to adjust.

I laid back and looked at the ceiling. I couldn't be in debt. I didn't want to be in debt- I needed to still give and be responsible. I needed to keep going and growing. I needed to not complain- and I found that even my silent complaints in my heart absolutely counted. I needed a mental rearrangement, an adjustment. A place where I needed to get up and go and grow.

I needed to have some courageous conversations. But I also needed to heal to make sure that I was equipped to have them and not bleed. Abba sat with me, and I told Him about all that was bothering me. That's how I had to approach things before I had to reach and speak to other people.

At that time, Abba really taught me the importance of waiting on His timing. I didn't want to be a bull in a china shop, but part of the reason why that happened was because I didn't know how to sit. Trauma and all sorts of things got in the way. It didn't excuse how I went about things- but it give me mercy for not having the understanding in what to do and how to do things.

Sometimes, it still stung.

But that meant, that I had more that I needed to learn going forward. Abba God covered me, but I had internal things that needed to be dealt with for the time being. I knew it was time for me to have my own things. I needed to have my own things- but it was time for me to steward what God gave me as well. He was Kind in this too- every time I bumped and got knocked down I'd readjust and get back up again. I began to learn how to pray and fast- and the best thing was how great a help it was. But if you think this level was something, just wait.

19

Arrange It

I didn't know that's how the day was going.

I sat, in the morning. I'd done some scripture reading- I was getting my morning routine together. The main problem- I didn't know how to situate it around God.

Now, He had me in a process to regain focus. The methods- were intense. Not intense because of cruelty, but intense because the who I was created to be, and needed to be in this season needed to go through this.

And it took some time for it to get through to me. Abba God sat there patiently, waiting as He watched more of the old me peel away. He sent me back to square one. There was part A, and Part B- but both of them were in relation to trauma and areas that needed to heal before I could move forward. Before we could move forward into all that He called me to be.

The place I was at was on the couch. Next to the wall. THAT wall. The wall that I spaced out staring at all those years ago before. The one that scared my dad- the one where I found out I had depression and anxiety. The one I would stare at for hours, before I was put on pills. That wall.

Now, it was the wall that I passed to get up in the morning. It was the wall I didn't stare at anymore.

I spent a majority of the past couple days cleaning. Deep cleaning- emptying childhood rooms. Having harsh conversations. Healing in places and spaces that I had encountered before- but this time for closure.

The trash bags were full. I spoke about wanting healthy help. I spoke up about abuse I had endured at a young age. I revisited those who mistreated me in my youth. The places where it happened. See- I'd forgiven the new ones. The new ones that came that I had forgiven, but I had been abused there too.

Abba God showed me something powerful here- how to get my voice back. How to use my voice- in love. To show His love for others. That rejection wasn't gripping me anymore, now that I knew Him, and who I was as His well beloved.

Being a marshmallow didn't upset me anymore. It turns out, Abba God loves marshmallows- especially when they're wise enough to discern their boundaries. Especially when the biggest boundary had to do with following what Abba God said. Being able to sit and listen, and speak. To giggle and laugh. To focus on Him.

Focusing on Him when there wasn't money or I wasn't sure what to do. Or how to do it. When God shattered my own personal limitations and definitions about what 'impossible' looks like to Him.

A hint, it means that nothing is impossible with Him. But that was key to all of this- Him.

Abba God giggled while I sneezed. I kept sneezing. I was throwing out trash, piles of old clothing. It's like He and I were in a time capsule, and I was running into a girl I hadn't been in years and would never be again.

The girl that was in this space was battered. Beaten. Bruised. Traumatized. When that girl left this space- she went to be homeless and to learn how to build herself into who she thought she was going to be. But there was one thing the Lord hadn't told me- and that's that I wasn't as equipped as I thought. It turns out, the wounds from the space, and other places were still with me. He knew this.

I hadn't found out.

Not until much, much later.

So now, here I was. Back in the same room a different woman that was still changing everyday.

I started the vacuum after sweeping the floor. The carpets were the same. I wiped down the door. I prayed and hummed- as I picked up old memories. They made the same noise hitting the side of the trashbag.

The accessories from old boyfriends- and the trauma that came from both sides of those relationships. Gone.

The grief from animals and pets.

Gone.

The baby box. I dusted it off- went through it. The small pliars, the sippy cup. I rid of the older things- the old wipes. The broken things. With each item I got lighter and lighter.

Abba God and I took a break. I exhaled- with a smile on my face. Those things had to go. It was time.

I looked back and the small items of things to go through. That's when I saw it.

That book.

The one that I picked up when I was transitioning from here to homelessness- to there. That one that started this conversation and dialogue between God and I. Between us getting to know each other- and us continuing to get to know each other. I'd read it years ago.

Maybe there were notes in there?

But the longer I looked at- the Lord sent a nudge in my spirit. It was time to read it again. Right now? No. Later today yes. It was time to go clean the kitchen.

Now the thing about cleaning the kitchen was this- while it was a place that the Lord and I spent time in, it was a place where I was hurt too. Where it was then told to me- that as a woman this was supposed to be my place. It was where I had to meet harsh expectations, it was a place where unforgiveness let bitterness and anxiety take root. But now that I thought about it- anxiety took root everywhere.

It was a place that was unfair.

Abba God glanced over to His shelf. You know, the one in heaven where He keeps record. He noted the location, and recalled the times that He stood in the kitchen with me. When my tears fell into the dishwater- and I'd pop bubbles with Him to smile again.

The tears caused in part, by the same person that God has motioned to have me temporarily stay. This wasn't going to be for an extended amount of time. Until another time that was appointed.

Okay.

For once, I wasn't in a rush.

The focus wasn't on getting out of the space- it was making sure I went through it and came out fully equipped.

I didn't want to despise small beginnings.

I was tired of me hitting some of the same walls- I needed to grow. I needed to learn how to keep going. How to keep growing and going. To know where, and when- and why and how. To get to know Abba God more. I hadn't experienced this side of Him this way, and I was tired of fighting to learn about how to do it. I was tired of learning about how I was weak, and not about how to apply the Lord's strength.

For the first time. I was intrigued to look at God's perspective of me. Even when He let me know- that was going to require an uncomfortable process. After fighting Him so much- I decided to yield.

Now the yield was hard. I was back from where I left.

Oh yeah, we needed to talk about that. About your pride.

Yeah. That was one thing that I didn't realize was as large as it was. One of the things that came to my attention was the role of pride in trauma. I didn't know it- but there was a shield. Though we made large strides in therapy, this area of pride had to be addressed this way.

I know I wasn't the biggest fan of Him going hard knocks- but being back here had me come to the realization that this was one of the first places that pride grew. Largely, in reaction to what I underwent here as a kid. Now, I needed to come back to figure out what in the world that last bit of pride was guarding so much in the first place. Now, when you sit down to genuinely think about we have to come to a realization. Pride guards trauma. Pain. Hurt- so usually when people have pride there's something like that underneath. So, when it comes to addressing pride it's important to note that calling them out for having pride will ONLY MAKE IT BIGGER. Instead- let them know it's a safe space. Pride can't do much against a safe space- that's when vulnerability really gains it's superpower.

I think the biggest thing, was the realization that there needed to be another conversation. It turns out, a lot of the people that had traumatized me in the past were growing up themselves. It was something incredible to say the least, but when we did hit those bumps (which we did) it was easier to stop and take a couple of steps back. Old me would have popped of, new me knew that it was necessary to speak in conversations to avoid the bombs from going forth. I didn't want things to get worse, but better.

If things got too bad, I'd say something. I would have that conversation. I'd speak about it. In fact, it was a blessing to use some of the therapy techniques that I knew of others.

One thing for sure, Abba God was making it easier to navigate this situation. When it came down to it- this was becoming something I thought less about- but became second nature.

Then there was the fact to see all the things that therapy had healed me from. And, I loved to find a way to navigate that conversation as well.

20

XIII

The first page had no writing.

Abba God and I sat with a pen. We were having a still day- but this was what He needed me to do next.

I scribbled.

Abba God let me know- that everything was about to make sense soon. My process was going to be on the next couple of pages. Did I know what that meant? No. Am I now aware of what that was going to mean?

Only because right when I read the first sentance- I felt Abba God remove the covering.

This book didn't read the same the second time.

The previously blank pages- they had scribbles on them. They were happening quickly. So quickly. Abba God sat with a smile. It's like years worth of puzzle pieces began to click into place.

Each click, my breathing became unsteady.

With each click, and letter- my eyes watered up a little bit more than they were before.

I tried to speak to the Lord about it- and I choked up a little bit more.

Here comes the marshmallow.

That's when there was another covering being removed with every page turn and every word. It was how this book was connected to my process the whole time. However, the time was simply not appointed.

Just then, a light sticky note fell out from the page. On it- handwriting. Handwriting from years ago- before that version of me left this place. It's like a past version had dropped in to say hello.

What struck me was this- one- how much the handwriting had changed. It's like someone made a time stamp about who I was. Abba God knew this version of me, and loved and covered her just the same. Now, it was time for us to re-meet. It was for a couple of seconds- but for a couple of seconds none the less.

She took one note.

Compared to what I had just written in the last couple of pages this seemed less. But. Abba God bumped me to let me know that what she needed in that season. The same way that I was going to need the notes- though new- to prepare where the Lord was taking me.

The light green sticky note went like this,

- Jesus is a confirmation and physical representation of not only God's word, but his character.
- We needed an increase in the next level of intimacy. Experience with Him shapes our belief.

That was it.

I smiled. I made a note saying hello to past me and allowing me to continue forward.

The funny, yet not so funny thing was when the Lord revealed this next portion. He was covering me from the fact that- I had left the fundamentals. Somewhere- there was more trauma that I had hit, I got comfortable puffed up and didn't act the same as I did back then.

My stomach dropped.

I'd been singing more often.

Abba God and I were closer. I knew that- there was something about humility that was missed during the expansion.

That's part of why we were back here.

Past me didn't take as many notes. She didn't highlight everything- she didn't know scriture as much as I did now- but her heart.

There was a reliance I had here, that I didn't have in the other places.

That's why He brought me back here. First to heal, and second- this elevation required a different foundation. A different structure. Then came the realization- this elevation was going to require that I have that foundation. But-the trauma had to be addressed. Which is why Abba God was walking me through all of this. That couldn't come with me- but the heart's position to Him on the sticky note did.

Just then- I came to an uncomfortable realization. Things were this way before I ran into all of the other people. I paused, and felt upset. Abba God uncovered that healed me- was going to have to advocate more on my behalf. I was doing better- but I was really going to have to be bold about this. Bold.

Now, I knew how to do it in love and keep my hands clean at the same time. At the end of the day- the process- was to build the character- but now it was time to make sure the foundation was set.

Wait.

No- part me of me was trying to be concerned about what other people thought. However, that meant that there was going to be another conversation. In part-one, this residue had to go. And it did. No one had me more committed to my process than the lover of my soul. That meant one thing- this was going to- and would be for an audience of one. There were people that were going to applaud me and others would pop up later.

The thing was Abba covered me through it. He knew hearts- and He let me know some genuinely made mistakes. Others, knew but that was how they felt about it. At the end of the day- no one was going to love me more than Him.

Which is why every page turn caused me to sit and take a bit more time with Him. We were going at His place. His time.

This was about Him.

And part of me- while I was in the pain space kept forgetting what that meant. Abba covered me when I didn't know that all pride was doing was trying to shield the pain behind it from getting touched. Pride didn't want me to heal. God did.

That's why we were where we were. It was time for that covering to come off as well.

21

t's Safe Marshmellow

It didn't feel safe.

It's like every time I made a step forward with the Lord the enemy was in the back waiting. Before I knew it- I found myself circling something I had strived so hard to get away from. That was survival mode.

Now, coming from survival mode the last time, there were a couple of things that the Lord has taught me. The first, survival mode was when I shut down certain parts of myself so others could flourish. I put down rest and relaxation- instead I would work. That was because I associated work and being able to provide for myself as survival. Survival mode had another term- hyper independence. Plus the fact that this range of survival mode came from me being vulnerable and not being met- meant that I was going through it.

I didn't want ot admit it all the way- but Abba knew my heart. He saw the tears. Between the financial strain, and the frustration that came from knowing that there was so much in me that was struggling to come out- I was angry.

I yelled it out in the car.

I had to repent because I swore. I'd been clean of that for months. But the Lord needed for me to know that me being able to express anger meant that I was healing.

Healing.

I needed to heal here. It was ironic because it's one of the places where I was hurt the most. Abba God knew things would be different, but I didn't at the time. It was something out of a movie. I sat with my bible- trying to articulate to God the pain and frustration I felt with Him.

With God, all things are possible. It was just at that moment- things felt impossible. So that meant that something inside of me was not matching up with the exterior. I felt so finite, and small. I knew I was made to take up more space- and that His strength is made perfect in my weakness.

So why do I still feel weak? I don't want to be lazy, or idle. I didn't want to waste time resting. I was beginning to have a hard time resting- I felt like napping meant that I was inviting poverty. So that made resting when I had a hard emotional day even harder. Healing had me on edge. I was going in circles with myself- when I studied everything quieted down. Everything was silent and moving in a better place and position. But outside of studying, I had to be honest. I didn't feel safe.

I knew I was safe with God- but I only wanted to be with Him and not anyone else because being safe with other people while getting stabbed wasn't a thing. People were mocking me- passive aggresivley- I didn't want to be on social media. Sometimes, I took my SD Card out of my phone.

What hurt was the fact that there had been so much gossip. Everyone knew what I was going through because I'd ask for help and wouldn't get it. It was go get government assistance. Dismissive.

It stung.

No one would apologize either. They'd shift their gaze, or try not to speak to me. I knew I still needed to show up, but Abba God let me know.

He was concerned.

Abba God wanted us to go somewhere else. Do something else and go be with Him. He didn't like the way I was being treated. He was furious. It felt like my environment was becoming more and more constricting- He was growing me- and I knew I needed to be elsewhere for a time.

He knew who was sitting, trying to and thinking they could take my position. He knew what was in the pews, He knew it all. He knew I was focusing on my cup, and that means that sometimes it's important for you to pull away and simply be with Him. I didn't want to be antisocial, but I could feel my body wanting to protect itself from any further cuts. This was the spiritual equivalent of blunt force trauma. I knew to turn the other cheek, and to stand up for myself- but He knew that as much as I warned the others, they weren't going to take it seriously.

That was the thing.

In order for Him to let them know that they needed to take it seriously, I needed to go away. Just He and I for some time. He didn't want me there. He could see the seeds from up there. He needed me away for the reap, He knew my heart wasn't going to be able to take it.

That's part of what made today so hard. The realization of the reap. I didn't want to be an idol. I wanted to be a voice that they listened to in order to heed the warning, but theydidn't respect me. I wasn't valued.

I felt dust gaining on my feet with every warning. Every- don't do that. But, I had to understand that everything that they would tolerate was creating a space where nasty things could flourish. But, they loved the taste. Even if Abba and I abhorred it.

It was heartbreaking.

I couldn't see that part, no wonder He wanted me out of the way for the reap.

He was tired of me thinking that I was small too. And, it was important that we had that. It was time for me and Him to go outside and be together. For a bit, and for a time. He needed me to know that I was safe with Him. Apart from Him, there was nothing that was going to be accomplished.

Which meant, that I needed to get outside of what was left of this comfort zone.

22

Nice Vs. Kind

There's something about a final detox that makes little to no sense.

First of all, how in the world was all this sitting in me? Is it possible that there's going to be another experience or note concerning this? How when and where?

I couldn't get up. I was down to the last couple of dollars in my account- I needed to sow seed. Which meant that I was going to have to be online.

Now, I can't speak about this next part, but let's just say the God was setting things in motion that had no way of being stopped. Part of me wept for those who mistreated me, while I felt anger rising. I was sick of my walk with God being mocked and misunderstood. I didn't like that those who bypassed process- were the ones who in the end knew and still wanted to set me up for failure.

I felt it, they thought they were going to leave me for dead. But, God said that it isn't so. This was the last level of breaking- there was a reason why I felt that warning when it came to the contents of my heart.

Abba God lifted the veil on something- that yes my beautiful heart is a blessing. But it's time to be kind, not nice. Nice didn't have boundaries. Nice was so understanding of others it left out protections for myself. Nice was part of the reason why I had so much trauma.

But Kind.

See, the Lord is Kind. But- the Lord is fair and has boundaries. He cannot be mocked, or mistreated. He is not mean, He's just. He's deserving. He's all that He needs to be- so even when others try to mistreat Him (or think that it's possible too). He sits in His character and knows that universal laws will keep things just and in alignment.

The same laws that were applicable to me.

The weep didn't finish- He had to come lift the weight off of me as I sang and danced. Things were locked in- and my nice heart couldn't take it.

My nice heart needed to grow up.

Now, what in the world was the difference between kind and nice? English- didn't do it justice.

So, I clicked on a computer tab. The realization of being left for dead shook me from a delusion into a reality- that people were banking on me being 'nice'.

But love, in First Corithians is Kind. It does not delight in evil, but rejoices with the truth. There was no delight here, because I came to realize the extent that I was not loved. The detox was from the heartbreak- the anger the frustration the realization.

Here's what I learned:

- Nice (Nechmad)- pleasant, agreeable, lovely.
- Kind (Chesed)- kindness with a deeper sense of love, compassion, and loyalty.

There's a difference between being lovely and being love. Lovely is external, being agreeable and pleasant doesn't mean that you're aligning yourself with things for your best interest. Or for what God has for you. Who are you agreeing with for the sake of being pleasant?

Now kind, I realized something. It's active, continuous- ongoing. A deep sense- that requires trust and vulnerability. Compassion- which is a strength when you apply it the correct way- action when deeply moved by something. Being kind requires thought, parameters...that's when it hit me.

Kindness has boundaries.

Boundaries that operate with that last word- loyalty. Abba God showed me that loyalty is a boundary maker. It shows who you serve, truly. For instance- love does not delight in evil- but it rejoices with the truth. That's a reflection of the loyalty of love- true love from the father delights in such things. The truth. His truth and care. His love. What He decides as law.

Then I had to realize the painful truth- my loyalties were not in alignment with God. In fact, some of the people I'd been serving needed me to be nice- because nice doesn't operate under loyalty the same way kindness does. Kindness has loyalty that's defined by boundaries, nice doesn't have boundaries. That's why people love when you're nice.

They have a problem when you're kind. Kindness means that there's parameters to what can be taken.

I spent years of my life being nice.

When I needed to be kind. When I needed to move in real love. Godly love. The love that makes Godly sense. He was setting me up to set me as the parameter- this was going to be so powerful. Yet, terrifying for those who thought that kindness was simply being nice. Kindness is saying- in love- that's not how God wants us to operate. Kindness is accountability. Kindness is strength, to stand and say no- not to condemn but to save those from stepping into dangerous places.

And at the end of being kind, whatever they did or did not heed was not on my hands. In the end- I was not to delight in evil- but to rejoice with the truth. Universal law would take care of the rest. If you're walking in God's love- you can't be mocked either.

Whoa.

Besides, I gave thanks to Abba God because this meant that all the setbacks were going to be for my favor anyway. The biggest thing the enemy was trying to do was weild people, God, and my flesh against me. There were some uncomfortable conversations that I needed to have with Him.

We had them.

So in the end- it all worked out. There was this part of me that needed to grow up. That was it. Now came to the conversation-

When it came to how I saw myself, was I going to be nice to myself- or kind?

Was I going to allow other people to be nice, or kind?

When it came to being all the God had called, and was calling me to be- was I going to be nice about it- or kind. Because love- rejoices with the truth. That nothing is impossible with God. That He's able to do EXCEEDINGLY, and abundantly above all that I can ask or think. That I am funded by the riches and glory in heaven. That His Word cannot return to Him void- that God cannot be mocked. So, what was holding me back from being all that God called me to be.

I was being 'nice about it'.

I wasn't being Kind.

Because if I was being Kind- the loyalty to God would have

removed all of the obstacles.

Oh.

I know the devil havin' a fit at this one LOL.

You know what was even more interesting? I began to have questions- and ended finding a little online therapist with some shorts to address the very issues that I was struggling with. With everyone, things became a bit clearer- and continued. I was able to have those difficult conversations with Abba God and myself.

He hadn't left me alone. In fact, He was close to me than ever. It came down to it- I really got tired of being shifted away from Him. Boundaries meant trauma, and difficulty reconnecting to Him. It meant that there was going to be additional people, places and things I was going to need to connect to. But at the end of the day, He knew what had happened to me and how I had been treated. He knew what I needed, and honestly though He covered me through all this- He wanted His babygirl back too.

There's something about being the creator of the universe, and everytime you go to reach for your shiny, there's more mud on it. You cant sit down with them- because they're shutting down at the fact that someone else mistreated them. You're sitting wanting a conversation-while they're navigating through other amounts of pain. Abba God covered me through all of this-but He was a little annoyed.

Perhaps, He could have been tired of this Grandpa! And indeed He was.

Now usually, I would remain in a stressed out state when it came to things such as these. But tonight, I was something completely different. This time- I was calm. Calm. I came to the realization that while I didn't enjoy the process of being at rock bottom- there was a need for me to be there. That's because- ther version of me that God wanted was only going to be accessible at this level.

The one where I couldn't rely on anything but Him. It took a couple of months- but I'll be honest with you. We were hitting turbo mode at the moment- because this stuff needed to come off of me. It really did.

And it was= in fact- a lot of me needed to grow up. I had to get myself together, in fact- in new ways the Lord hadn't run by me before. Did you know, part of the reason that I was having issues with putting down tech, wasn't just an addiction issue- but a lust issue? Now that was perplexing, I thought that lust and I had parted ways long ago. While not fornicating was a positive- I didn't know that it can also be part of what fuels you to have comfort outside of God.

No one ever told me that. It turns out, addiction, lust, and idolatry are far more connected than I knew.

I kept the SD card out of my phone for that very, and exact reason. It turns out, eating and overeating were connected to lust too. I still had me a lust issue- and while it had weakened in my gut- it was time to throw that thing out as much as possible. I drank more water and went to read my scriptures- this meant one thing. And, one thing alone- whatever Abba God just pointed out was not trying to go without a fight. So- that was something - this was part of the discipline and part of the push. I needed to get out of a comfort zone that lust had been locking me into. There's a reason why I kept hitting certain walls, and this was one of the main culprits. Whew.

23

Get Up and Build

I fell asleep when I should have gotten up in the morning again.

I sat up, from another dream. Had to bind, rebuke and cancel another round of enemy attacks. I said good morning to Abba God- and then my mind started to get cloudy.

I felt myself getting upset, then I started to sink a bit.

Now, I'll be honest with you.

I was sick of sinking- I don't deserve to sink. Then I remembered the external things, and internal things that kept trying to cause me to shrink. I was furious, angry, upset with what was going on.

But I was too set back into thinking again. Worse, it felt like when I took another step forward- I ended up taking multiple steps backward.

Just then I went to scroll a bit on my phone, and ran into a meme. One that let me know this wasn't an excuse.

I needed to stop thinking about how I could of been helped.

I needed to stop thinking about what could have been.

I needed to stop thinking about how things could have gone, as that was a snare. It was important to focus on the now, and

Abba God in it.

So it's important for there to be a foundation going forward with what needs to be done.

I don't want you to look at what you can't do.

Look at what you can do.

Honestly, it felt like that hurt even worse. I wasn't sure what was left of the comfort zone but this had to be one of them. But what came up with this one- was sheer disdain. I didn't like something about this.

That's because something in me was growing. It was the ability to remain focus despite the negative things that were going on in life. Or, what I thought was negative.

Turns out- since nothing is impossible with God- that's means that all things are indeed possible.

So I statres at a screen. the 72 cents in my bank account and said- Here goes nothing.

And that's when I took step number one.

People might mock me, but at the end of the day; this was going to be for an audience of One. People were going to be ticked- but this was one of the first times in my life where I didn't care about what other people think. Or what they thought. Or what they could think.

I cared about what Abba God thought.

I cared about accomplishing His purpose in the earth. I felt a way about the obstacles and cruelty I had faced- but at the end of the day- God was going to respond to my faith. That's because, without faith- it's impossible to please God. It was time to get serious about everything that God said about me. It was important to speak about this- and to note this.

What was I doing upset when the Creator of the Universe was in my corner? He made the corner, so nothing in the corner was going to be bigger than me. Greater is He who is in me, than He who was in the world anyway. I wanted to serve, but my appetite for abuse and mistreatment was not there. I had a 'no' (in love of course) that was ready to go at any given time.

Love doesn't allow that.

Love doesn't do that.

Love won't let you do that.

And I was comfortable enough to sit- I didn't want to people please. I wanted to make a space. One in love, where love was. Genuine love, genuine serving- people with pure hearts and clean hands that would reach their God given potentials. Where rejection and pain was left at the door- no mocking no struggle. That was the build. That's what needed to be cultivated.

Every painful experience meant one thing. It was a reference point for later. Someone out there needed to meet love and empathy that they didn't recieve in the same spaces and places. Someone needed a safe place to meet Abba God too- even it if was only through a smile and conversation.

At that moment, I came to the realization.

The solution that Abba God needed to do this was me. People needed to learn how to love- how to heal. How to grow- even when everyone counted them out. But there was something that I realized. That Abba God uncovered just as I was writing this.

They didn't know that Abba God was in their corner. But I did.

So why was I down?

He needed me as an example, to not only show how to stand up- but how to have God be the strength in their weakness.

A force. An experience.

Me.

In that moment, there were no more excuses. Did I believe what God said about me?

Did I?

Did I believe, who He said I was?

Did I believe everything that He said.

It didn't matter who came to cut, or poke or prod. Did I love God enough, to be all that He called me to be? In all situations, even in the fair or seemingly unfair- it wasn't unfair. He was there, I had a voice. I had more choices that I had known. That's why I needed to heal, to use my voice to place boundaries- to learn about these things to teach others.

Vulnerability- was absolutely going to be my superpower. It is. Being love. Being gentle, kind, patient, compassionate, beautiful. I was made to have clean hands and a pure heart- is that not the cause to build and move things for Him? Did I care about being righteous, and having clean hands at all times? Did I have the faith to maintain them- even when the world would say, that I had every right to swing.

Did I not trust that no matter what Abba God had my back. Did I trust Him to keep moving?

I felt the tears welt up when I realized that the answer was yes. It was the first time I realized, the other things didn't matter. They wouldn't matter- people needed the real me. The process, the pace- all of it. So when I entered into that room- they knew I did the self investment.

They had a template. A paradigm. Abba God literally gave them a walking gift to show them- I love you this much too.

That was the point of the covering. That was the point of the Lord being Kind- so I can learn how to be Kind like Him too. It took all that time just to get that one point. The bumps, the prods, the falls, the difficulties, the struggles, the cruelty- it was never going to be strong enough to change Him. Which meant, it wasn't going to be great enough to change me.

I got my butt up and built.

I was sick of me getting in my way, and I was sick of other people and situations pushing buttons and having an effect. So when it all came down to it- that meant that there were other things that needed to get knocked out.

This was for an audience of One, and this time I was taking things seriously. For sure. Taking me seriously, and praying about what in the world I needed to do in order to be serious about it.

"I'll cover you during this too."

This time, Abba God let me know- for the next steps be sure to be Kind.

I had to think about it- and came to the realization that being Love- was actually more powerful and complex. When God is Love, and then you're love- but it's a powerful thing to be too. Because of that- Abba God is right. It's important to be Kind.

Because if I was going to be honest, it was going to take a lot time with Abba God to have the strength to be Kind. That's the important thing to remember- that being Kind was going to require me being closer to Him than I'd been. But not as close as I'd ever be.

He said He'd cover me during that process too. But, I'd need to remember this in order to be kind to myself and others. It's a tall order- but Abba God built me for it. And that's something I needed to remember- that covering of grace is necessary. That's for sure.

Look, there was something else that we needed to talk about. First and foremost- I came to see some of the details of the build.

Abba God wasn't just coming after the mental and emotional. Abba God was coming after the physical. Now at first- things were okay but then we had to get to the point where we really needed to get up and push.

We had to have that flesh vs. the spirit conversation. Now, here's the thing about the flesh and the spirit. Yes- them things are quite contrary to one another. Beyond contrary. But what I found was that once my spirit man got fit, even my physical flesh began to struggle. Honey.

This was the part that needed to be spoken of- my physical stamina. Along with me taking care of myself. When it came down to it- my physical care needed work. In order to carry what the Lord needed me to do- and where He needed to go- I had to keep going. I had to keep going forward and pushing and my flesh wasn't fighting me to go backward. My flesh was navigating the effects of the new push. His strength was and is still made perfect in my weakness so I pushed forward.

Then there came what came with the physical stamina. I'm telling you- there's something that needs to be stated and said. It's not just working out. But writing, reviewing, thinking- I needed to go to God for even more fill ups. This was a new act- I wouldn't call it a balancing act though. Because, outside of my relationship with God there was nothing I wanted to balance with Him. Talk about growth. I wanted Him first, and the rest would fall in line and be in order. That's what was the most important. It came down to being for an audience of one. Of only One.

Now, that meant that there were things that I thought were ready but weren't. I had to step out in faith- and on faith. I had to step through on faith at the instructions. We needed this step- but it turns out that it was bigger. So, what do we do? That means that we need to speak and to have a conversation.

No, not this one. Build this right now, and then build the other things later. I had to shift in obedience. I had to shift and do and speak and execute in obedience. I had to learn how to make it all yield. And Abba God covered me in this. In the check ins. In the not check ins. In the prayer, in the praise, in the worship- in the moving. I found that the more we built- the more aggressive I became about navigating certain areas and conversations. I learned that the more that I built- the more I had to run to Him to be refueled. The more that, that cornerstone- became a cornerstone.

Honestly, part of the reason behind building this book is to reveal Jehovah Rapha as the one who covers me. The one who heals. The one who continues to heal- but even in the construction of this I had a covering. He covered the fact that I was writing about my process- that was still processing. Now that I think about it- I wonder if the angel in heaven keeping record about was smiling in the same parts that I did.

He was healing me into the person that's built to carry this. That's built to carry this thing- that's built to carry this thing forward. But the wildest part- is that no matter how much I physically built myself- God was still going to carry more weight than I was. And in His goodness and His grace- He covered me until my mind was healed enough to comprehend. The more that I built physical strength, my dependence on Him was going to have to be even more. Even more. Even greater.

I situated the construction hat. Abba God glanced over with a smile on His face. There was no limitation with Him. The same way that there would be no limitation in Him. The same way nothing is impossible with God- meant that all things were possible. All things are possible- and He covered me until I was able to get to that point.

What about the naysayers? The ones who counted me out- before, when I wasn't healed, it mattered to me. It did. But- that was precious brainpower that I needed to invest in me. To build in me. To move on behalf of the Lord for me. What if someone didn't think I was an original?

How you going to tell the manufacturer that you don't think you're an original? I spent too much time there. Too much time in self preservation. Entirely too much time in self preservation to tell you the truth. Why?

That part of my mind needed to heal. See- part of me thought safety was a feeling. Abba God sat with me through the process- and taught me that safety isn't a feeling. Safety is a choice. Fear is a feeling, and it's not something that from His Kingdom. I found myself operating in fear so long that once it came up and out, once it came forward Jehovah saw a gap that I didn't. I needed to heal, because my relationship with fear needed to be nonexistent. But, as long as I didn't heal it would always find a way to have a space.

The only way it was going to go was when I healed. When I got that real understanding of love. The kind of love- where perfect love would cast out fear. The fact that Abba God is love- and since Abba God is love that means that fear had no place this entire time. So- this part of the build- yes indeed this part of the build was the character of Jehovah Rapha doing an overhaul. He, in His kindness at first did it quietly. Then He grew- I received a little more push back. Then came something even more incredible- the fact that parts of me were pre-programmed to function without fear.

So-that was confusing. But Abba God let me know something. That fear factor wasn't in my predetermined settings- the trauma shifted things around. This wasn't something that was in my nature. It wasn't intended for this to be in my nature. Not at all. And yet- for so long I held on to fear as if it had the ability to protect me more than Abba God did. But it didn't. And, it couldn't. And- it wouldn't. Abba God was using Rapha to cover me. And the crazy part is- He was looking at a version of me He never intended to exist- but it did not stop Him from loving me. That's when it hit me. That I needed to do better. I needed to be better. He had already given me the capacity to be all that He had called me to be. I was the one stalling.

There were mental limitations that were left. One's that were there from the trauma and voids that were preventing me from going forward to be all that the Lord called me to be. The block to the build, were the things that I didn't want to address with Him. They were the things that were hard, that were difficult- that were complicated. But then came the question- well Lord if you had me go through all of that then it was for some reason right?

Ding. Ding. Ding.

It was a small store. My cart and I were scooting around.

"Do you need help with anything?"

"No thank you."

I sat on the floor and shuffled a couple of things around. Until I overheard they needed help locating something.

Oh I know where that is- let me go help.

We both stood there, and hey- I took the opportunity to chat. You never know what someone might be going through. Long story short, I ended up with a cart containing items that I didn't intend to buy- and a coat with tears on it. I didn't care about the tears. I cared that someone out there took the time to care. Abba God made them too, He had a plan- and you know what? Maybe someone needed to take the time to find out that Abba God's character of Jehovah Rapha cares about them too.

Well today, they did.

And honestly- I needed to know this too. The volume of the book that's been written about me- it may look a bit like this one. It may not. I'll be honest with you- it might not be all roses and things. As I have not been those things either. But- once thing is that Abba God already knew and had the idea of what He needed me to accomplish. He set it already. So- to tell you the truth the real question became, how could I help others do the same? That day was the answer. I got it.

24

This time- It Wasn't Me.

A turning point.

You know what's so incredible about a turning point? Or about this one in particular? I didn't even know I was in it.

This was the part where the Lord showed how much He healed me.

The phone rang.

It was ringing.

Then there was a hello.

Now- I'm not going into detail about it. But, it had come to my attention the extent that people took when it came to taking advantage of me. This phase of my life was indeed vulnerable to say the least. I found myself in a state of helplessness that some may take the opportunity to try and have advantage of.

Abba God and I were at a similar crossroad that I found myself. The one where the same question arises- are you going to speak about it or are you going to shut down? Shutting down was second nature to survival mode. The fawn the 'keeping the peace'- but this part of my life was beginning to look different. This was the part where the connection of love and boundaries was distinct.

It took time to get to this point. I cried- feeling the layers of trauma and resentment from of being a 'nice' person. The 'nice' person that abandoned their inner thoughts and feelings for the emotions of others. The one who had toxic empathy, and kept trying to find ways to keep the peace. But- the peace wasn't peaceful. In fact, the peace still had chaos in it because it didn't address the root and core functioning issues at hand. The 'nice' me wanted fake peace.

No.

Today- was the day that things were going to shift. I sat, inhaled and exhaled- took the time to breathe. My body wasn't tensing- it was calm. I knew the importance of keeping my composure in this moment.

How were the usual triggers and trauma buttons?

Jehovah Rapha got to them.

They were healed.

The didn't itch. They weren't flaring.

It didn't mean that the other person at the end of the line wasn't ready to touch them.

"No."

Then came the entitlement. The 'but I've helped you-so I deserve to treat you this way.' Next were the word curses. The jabs.

They didn't land.

They didn't hit.

The less of a reaction, the angrier they would get. Past me

would have reacted- but the version sitting here in this space knew better. The girl here knew her identity. Her identify in the Lord. His Kindness. How He covers her. She knew Jehovah Rapha had been here, and now the others would know too.

"I'll just hang up the phone then."

"Goodbye." It was calm.

Then the line clicked.

With that, I felt the timidity I had come to carry all of those years fall to the floor. I felt everything shift, and shake. I felt a new breath come out of me-freedom. A new freedom. A voice. One that was new, that I hadn't used before- and one that brought a smile to Abba God's face.

My hands weren't shaking. My stomach didn't flip. Anxiety didn't even get a chance to rear it's ugly head against me. It was something new. Something big- something important. This was the me hiding under all those layers of trauma and pain.

She was bold, assertive, loving above all- and more importantly, she was solid on what God said about her. I rose and threw those word curses to the ground in Jesus name. They weren't going to cover me. They weren't my identity, instead I wrapped myself in the scripture of the one who covers and heals me.

This was the strength. This was the growth. This was me being secure in my God-given identity. In my dominion, in my authority- the one He gave me back in Genesis. The same authority that mankind has over the earth- wrapped with that key phrase- "In Jesus Name." See, this is what was so incredible about accepting Christ as your Lord in savior- is that you have the same level of impact that He has on this earth.

You align yourself into your full God- given identity. You decide the day that you're going to have. You tell the enemy what he can and cannot do. You learn about boundaries and parameters- some of the most fundamental concepts in the book of Genesis.

Not today.

It was important for me to say this. For the longest time- I'd been suppressed from many things I didn't know how to heal.

There were other attempts that week- the devil was MAD he couldn't press the same buttons. I sat in silence, in peace. I knew what did and did not deserve my attention. I knew that any wrongs I received, Abba God saw them too. Abba God took the time to admire His external handiwork- with a smile on His face.

There she is.

The one who knows the power of walking in the spirit- the one that knows the power of walking in love. The one who understands the difference between being kind, and being nice. The one that is gentle- the one that doesn't like the feeling of her flesh wanting to act up. The one who knows that no one is able to take her power without her permission. The one who knows how to get her power back.

At this moment, and perhaps only at this moment- Abba God's character trait of Jehovah Rapha pulled the (at the time) most powerful version of me from the weights of my past. The resilience, the drive, the strength- the pressure had turned me into a diamond. A diamond with focus as sharp and directed as flint.

Abba God sat with me. Things flowed out of me at a pace that I had not witnessed before. Rejection didn't feel or hit the same.

It couldn't. The shield of faith that the Lord gave me sent those arrows right into the pit. The trauma buttons, those triggers? They broke.

Shattered.

Were obliterated.

Destroyed.

And in that moment, it dawned on me. The power of Abba God. Jehovah Rapha was one portion of His personality- but this part of Him restores. He restores to the original design, the template of you when you were in your mothers womb. At the point- Abba God restored me into a version of myself that was the closest reflection of Him that I had seen at the moment. But, it was not the stopping point. We were just getting started. But in this moment, I understood the power of being who He made. How it took me so long, to be able to comprehend me. That in the end, the pain, the trauma the weapons- didn't have to impact my ability to love. How can darkness remove the light that's in you?

John 1:5 states that. "The light shines in the darkness and the darkness has not be able to overcome it."

Which means, that no darkness I could ever experience would be able to remove the light in me. The most the enemy could do was try to dim it and the Lord still covered me.

That's because of Him.

His mercy.

Grace.

Love.

Kindness.

Now, it's His time to shine.

25

A (Slight) Benediction

One of the many great things about the Lord is that He's all in. He guaranteed that He was all in with the sacrifice of Jesus Christ. So when you accept Christ, Abba wants to give you all that intimacy without boundaries. Abba wants intimacy, to hear about your day, to walk with you to class, and whatnot. The process of becoming who you are in Christ Jesus is a PROCESS. The Lord has already given you all the tools you need to walk it out, but you've got to walk.

Learning how to walk when you're used to being still is a skill in itself. You have to learn about what things have you thinking that comfort and stagnation that is a barrier to you walking with God.

The wildest thing about it- was figuring out how to adjust to the purity of his love as a process. But He will be with you every step of the way- because those personal adjustments and acknowledgments of barriers can get rough. When you're used to thinking you're alone or being in survival mode- this is one of the hardest things that you have to do. No one wants to have the conversations about getting out of survival mode- because oftentimes people spend their entire lives in it.

Here's encouragement, and the truth- He knows you have a journey. We're still on mine- and He knows that this will be for my earth life and eternity- and He is behind it 100 percent. I am, too. Every day, I learn the love language of God a little bit better. With all the choices I have in my free will, I still choose him. And that is what matters to Abba the most. This is a healthy relationship, so keep continuing and growing- every day, you are farther from the starting point than you were yesterday. I know that with all the choices I have of my free will, I still choose Him. That is what matters to Abba the most. Keep on growing and going- you've got places to be. And, if for any reason or instance you think that you can't make it through here- just know.

He's a redeemer of time.

Do you have breathe in your body and air in your lungs? Then you have time.

Thank you for taking the time to share this journey with me. I pray that you find how Abba God, and His character of Jehovah Rapha- wants you to be all that you can be. He made you. You're going to make it- just stay close to Him.

www.ingramcontent.com/pod-product-compliance
Lightning Source LLC
LaVergne TN
LVHW091316150826
845673LV00006B/1669

* 9 7 9 8 8 9 5 8 7 6 4 9 7 *